Sink or Swim

Sink or Swim

Stress Management Strategies to Ensure Your Survival

Joanne Steed-Takasaki with Jayme Pierringer

iUniverse, Inc.
New York   Bloomington

The information, ideas, and suggestions in this book are not intended as a substitute for professional advice. Before following any suggestions contained in this book, you should consult your personal physician or mental health professional. Neither the author nor the publisher shall be liable or responsible for any loss or damage allegedly arising as a consequence of your use or application of any information or suggestions in this book.

iUniverse books may be ordered through booksellers or by contacting:

iUniverse
1663 Liberty Drive
Bloomington, IN 47403
www.iuniverse.com
1-800-Authors (1-800-288-4677)

Because of the dynamic nature of the Internet, any Web addresses or links contained in this book may have changed since publication and may no longer be valid. The views expressed in this work are solely those of the author and do not necessarily reflect the views of the publisher, and the publisher hereby disclaims any responsibility for them.

ISBN: 978-1-4401-6427-9 (sc)
ISBN: 978-1-4401-6426-2 (ebook)

Printed in the United States of America

iUniverse rev. date: 10/28/09

Table of Contents

Foreword

Writing a book can be a difficult task. That task becomes even more difficult when your co-author is your daughter and best friend. Take this complication and multiply it when the two of you are living in different countries and both leading hectic lives. The times when we did manage to come together with good intentions for writing, the distractions were numerous and not limited to shopping, visiting, cooking, hitting the gym, and just plain hanging out. Last on that list of items was to sit down and channel our minds as we brainstormed new ideas for this book.

Through some miracle, we made it. We hope that our efforts will benefit you in some way, and we hope the love we have for this topic and the sense of urgency we feel to get this information to as many people as possible will be apparent.

Introduction

In more than twenty-five years of working in the educational field I have met many incredible individuals who have achieved personal and professional success but who feel they are lacking balance in their lives. No one knows better than a teacher what real stress is, so I can definitely relate. As I worked toward my master's degree in education, I focused heavily on research in the area of stress.

After many of my speaking engagements, I would have numerous people approach me about their issues with stress and how important it was that this topic be addressed. From there I began to understand the real need that existed for education about the stress response and strategies that we can use to bring balance back into our lives. I began Josta Consulting, Inc. because of this knowledge. Since its inception I have had the opportunity to present extensively in both business and educational settings, and I have worked with such clients as the Mirage Hotel and Casino and the Monte Carlo Hotel and Casino in Las Vegas. I found that I carried a deep passion for health and wellness, and I began my mission to help others achieve knowledge, balance, and success in their lives.

I have relied heavily on my daughter for support, whose degree in organizational behavior and human relations has primarily prepared her for a career path that would involve motivating and understanding what people want. Jayme found that so much of work and school life hinged around the ideas that we had discussed so frequently during our research on stress. As she has worked with MicroBusiness Mentors providing small business training and financial services among members of the low-income Hispanic community in Provo and surrounding areas, her understanding of our ideas has become even more concrete. MicroBusiness Mentors is largely a volunteer-based organization that works efficiently or inefficiently, depending on the level of motivation and desire of the volunteers. The best way to help employees and volunteers become deeply involved and work to their potential is not to offer monetary or external incentives but to provide new knowledge and tools to help address the daily changes and challenges in an ever-evolving workplace.

The true inspiration for this book came down to a simple idea: **We feel stress. Every day we feel stress.** There have actually been times in our lives when we have felt like we were drowning in stress. The authors of this book wanted to know everything we could about this important concept, and, more importantly, we needed to understand how we could use this knowledge in our own lives and to help others in their life struggles.

Our extensive research on this topic has taken us on a journey of discovery, a journey of knowledge, and a journey of healing. Our goal in this book is to share with you insights on the stress response, information about your body's reactions to stress, and specific strategies to help you keep your head above water.

Chapter 1: Sink or Swim

Life is meant to be lived.

—*Eleanor Roosevelt*

Imagine you do *not* know how to swim, and a friend pushes you in the deep end of a swimming pool. What do you do? What are you feeling? What are you thinking?

Well, when you pop up out of the water you probably experience feelings of panic. You most likely think you are going to drown, and you probably thrash about aimlessly in an attempt to keep your head above water. You might also call out to anyone who will listen in a desperate cry for help to save you.

Now imagine the same scenario if you *do* know how to swim. What do you do? What are you feeling? What are you thinking? Well, this time when you pop up out of the water you more likely experience feelings of frustration or anger at your friend, but your training kicks in, and you easily tread water while you catch your breath. The thought of drowning probably doesn't even enter you mind because you have learned exactly what to do in these situations. There is no aimless thrashing, no desperate cry for help. Just a few seconds to compose yourself and then a calm, controlled swim to the side of the pool.

Now think of when you are faced with a stressful situation—a situation that initially seems to be more than you are able to handle. Do you experience feelings of panic? Do you tell yourself you are going to drown in this mess? Do you figuratively thrash around aimlessly just trying to keep you head above water? Do you feel like crying out in a desperate attempt to get help?

Just as swimming lessons can give you the confidence to remain calm in the pool, gaining an understanding of the stress response, analyzing your reactions to stress, and learning strategies to deal with

1

your stress can help you feel the same calm control in your life when things go wrong.

What Do We Know about Stress?

Stress is definitely not something new. In 1932 Walter B. Cannon, a physiologist at the Harvard Medical School, described the body's reaction to stress, and in 1956 Dr. Hans Selye of the University of Montreal was able to specify the physiological changes in the body due to stress. Selye recognized the need for people to make informed choices about handling the stress of life.

Since that time, a vast amount of research has been and is being carried out in this field. All of us, and especially those of us in professions known for high levels of stress and burnout, have an obligation to find out more about this important subject. How do we go about this? How do we begin to handle this thing we call stress that tears through our emotions, causes discomfort in our relationships, and depletes our immune systems? Paula Jorde Bloom in her book *Avoiding Burnout: Strategies for Managing Time, Space, and People in Early Childhood Education* wrote:

> Our challenge in managing stress . . . is to gain as many insights as possible into the correlation between stress and performance in our own lives. Only then can we begin to reengineer our behavior and our environment to use stress to our advantage, benefiting from its positive aspects while minimizing its negative ones.

Our Need for "Eustress"

Overall, stress is receiving bad publicity. We seem only to hear about stress in a negative context. It is valuable to understand that we need some stress to lead successful and challenging lives. Stress that produces personal growth or spurs us on to accomplish our goals is called "eustress," a term coined by Hans Selye. Eustress is good stress, and it serves several important purposes. Stress protects us and gives us a mechanism for dealing with threats, and it provides us with the adrenaline necessary to play sports, write exams, and follow our passions and dreams. Stress adds anticipation and excitement to our lives. T. Harv Eker, in his book

Mastering the Secrets of the Millionaire Mind, states, "Being comfortable may make us feel warm and fuzzy, but it doesn't allow us to grow. The only time you are actually growing is when you are out of your comfort zone." And stress definitely nudges—or in some cases yanks—us out of our comfort zones.

One of my passions is working in the fitness industry as a personal trainer where I see the positive effects of stress continually. If individuals want to increase their muscle size, they must apply resistance to that muscle in order for it to grow. If they want to enhance their cardiovascular systems, they must be stressed in order to progress. However, this stress needs to be carefully planned in order to have maximum benefits. Just the right amount of stress can create beautiful biceps! Too much stress (or over training), however, can have negative effects on the body. Similarly, you do not grow emotional or intellectual "biceps" without resistance or adversity. And similarly, too much stress or adversity without proper coping techniques can also have adverse effects.

The Stress Response

In understanding stress, it is important to have a fundamental knowledge of the way our bodies respond to stress. In the 1920s, Walter B. Cannon established the "fight or flight" description of stress. Simply put, when we encounter stress in our lives, our sympathetic nervous system immediately prepares for fight or for flight by creating such bodily responses as an increased heart rate, increased sugar and fat levels, reduced intestinal movement, dilated pupils, increased perspiration, decreased blood clotting time, and constricted blood vessels. (The sympathetic nervous system could be compared to the gas pedal in your car.) Primitively we would have run away from or fought our stress enemy, and this expelled energy would have caused our parasympathetic nervous system (the brakes) to take over and return our bodies to homeostasis.

Modern stressors, however, are often psychological rather than physical, but our bodies do not make this distinction. Therefore our sympathetic nervous systems activate our stress response when things go wrong at work, at home, or in our relationships. Because our bodies are designed to react physically to stress—say by running away or fighting the enemy—our parasympathetic nervous system does not activate, and our bodies remain stuck in a hyper-vigilant state. Over time, the repeated activation of the stress response without action takes a heavy toll on the physical body. It can cause damage to our cardiovascular systems, suppress our immune systems, and actually increase our vulnerability to everyday pressures and mental problems. Researchers now believe that most if not all illnesses are related to unrelieved stress.

The goal to maintain health is to find ways to activate our parasympathetic nervous systems and bring our bodies back to homeostasis when dealing with our stressful lives. Achieving a better balance in life is the key. We need to find a behavioral balance, an intellectual balance, a spiritual balance, an emotional balance, and a physical balance in our lives. I use the acronym BISEPS (with an S) because I am a personal trainer, and I believe achieving balance gives us cause to "flex our BISEPS."

Behavioral balance involves eliminating detrimental stress management behaviors and replacing them with healthy, positive behaviors. Intellectual balance involves learning to understand and harness the incredible power of our minds. Spiritual balance allows us to become more self-aware—learning more about ourselves, our strengths, our weaknesses, our purpose for being here. Emotional balance comes from releasing ourselves from unnecessary emotional burdens and freeing ourselves to form healthy, supportive relationships in our lives. And physical balance is achieved by targeting activities that have an actual physical effect on our bodies—activities that counteract the stress response. On the following page is a simple five-part model that illustrates these concepts.

Please join me, and in the following chapters I will discuss specific strategies for you to incorporate into your life so that you can learn the "lessons of stress" and design a plan to get you "swimming" your way to a more balanced, stress-enhanced life.

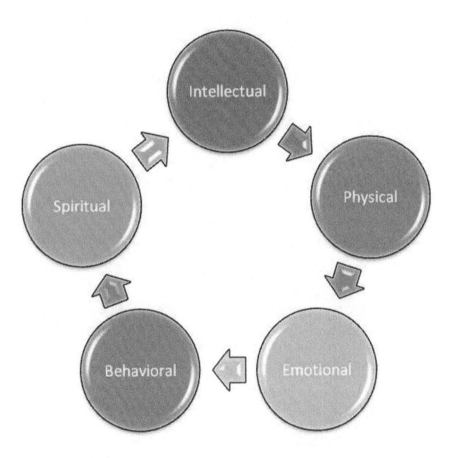

Achieving Balance in Your Life

Chapter 2: Get Rid of the Extra Baggage

Above all, we cannot afford not to live in the present. He is blessed over all mortals who loses no moment of the passing life in remembering the past.

—*Henry David Thoreau*

With the new airline restrictions on luggage, and the amount of flying that we do, we have become quite aware of exactly what we are packing around in our suitcases. Some items are lightweight and easy to take along—you can carry lots of these items and your suitcase still comes in under weight. And some items are very heavy and cumbersome—one or two of these can put you over the limit very easily. What if these same restrictions applied to your life baggage? You could carry around lots of love, joy, and optimism—they weigh very little. But you must rid yourself of things like worry, jealousy, and anger. They are very heavy items and quickly drag you down and extol high costs from your life journey.

Sheri Dew is the president of a large publishing company in the United States. In her book *If Life Were Easy It Wouldn't Be Hard*, she tells the story of arriving in New York City late one evening for a crucial meeting the next morning. At 3:00 a.m. the fire alarm in her hotel went off. Instead of bolting out the door, a moment of vanity overcame her. If she couldn't get back into the hotel before her meeting, she would need to look presentable and prepared. So she grabbed her suitcase and her briefcase before heading out the door. When she got into the fire escape she realized she was the only person carrying her luggage—all 40 lbs. of it. She also became painfully aware that her room was on the forty-fourth floor. Of course her journey to safety was grueling and exhausting. Somehow she made it down but at a high price. She was recovering from knee surgery on her left knee, and the flight shredded her right knee. The moral of the story? When you have to evacuate your hotel room, leave your baggage behind!

Sheri Dew's trip down forty-four flights of stairs has some interesting parallels to our journey through life. It was scary, grueling, and painful, and at times she felt like she couldn't keep going. Sound familiar? But the trip didn't have to be as hard as she made it; what if she had just left her baggage behind?

Socrates tells us that an unexamined life is not worth living. Sometimes we complicate our lives by dragging our baggage along with us, and our emotional and spiritual joints take a pounding because of it. What might we be unnecessarily carrying along in our life suitcases? Worry, jealousy, guilt, unforgiving hearts, anger, regret, pride, resentment, the desire to retaliate, fear, insecurity—any of these sound familiar? How full is your suitcase? Often in life we cannot choose what happens to us, but we do choose our baggage. Perhaps, as Socrates suggests, we need to examine our baggage today and resolve to travel a little lighter.

Most of us are carrying around heavy burdens in our hearts and minds, and we must find ways to move beyond them. Our negative thoughts and past memories can often gain power over us and take over us completely. Some of us must deal with horrifying, haunting regret. Some of us carry with us the shame of abuse, the disappointment of unfulfilled dreams, guilt in raising our children, and the list goes on. We limit ourselves by living in the past and must strive constantly to be truly present in the moment rather than letting ourselves be lured into past pain. Our burdens can be like a dark storm gathering momentum inside us with each negative thought or each new painful experience penetrating our emotional defense shields. Sometimes these storms can silently gather force for years and even lifetimes if we allow them. And if they go unchecked our bodies will ultimately pay the price. It is important to remember that these storms are only fed by negativity. Gratitude, positive interactions with others, and inspirational and uplifting conversations and thoughts will not feed the storm but will rather start to disperse its power and force.

Now of course this may not be as easy as it sounds. Many of our burdens are difficult to overcome on our own and may require studying, seeking professional help, applying long-term consistent effort, or finding the deeper cause of burdens to truly eliminate them from our lives. It is important that we own and take responsibility for our baggage. It is easy to blame others or circumstances for our unhappiness or failure to achieve and succeed fully in our lives, but ultimately we become responsible for our own destinies. Let's take a closer look at some of these burdens.

Worry

The first step to release ourselves from our burdens and lighten our baggage is to acknowledge the burdens we carry and to desire to let go of them. Worry often haunts us on a daily basis. Many times we feel that if we worry about our problems, our families, our situations, then we will be better prepared to deal with them. In reality our worry doesn't help us have more control over the situation, or lessen our pain in dealing with difficult problems. We face the hurt and disappointment once just worrying that something may happen and then again if our worries actually come true. It is important to realize the difference between being proactive in areas like emergency preparedness and just plain worrying. Having an emergency food supply in case of a natural disaster or a fire evacuation plan in case of a fire is different than worrying each time your spouse leaves the house that he or she will be in a car accident or suffer a stroke, or worrying daily that you will some day be diagnosed with cancer. If you are a worrier, try this formula. After you have acknowledged your worries, write them down and then apply these questions:

1. What would happen if I quit worrying about these things?

2. Am I psychic? Can I really predict the future or read people's minds?

3. Is it possible I am exaggerating the situation?

4. If I think realistically, what is the probability of my worry actually coming true?

5. What are some situations that would be more likely to happen?

6. Do I know other people who have dealt with the situation I am worrying about and made it through?

7. What coping skills can I use to handle what I fear might happen? Could I change my thinking about difficult situations and adopt the attitude that adversity can be a positive thing, can make us rise to new heights and achieve a new level of strength and empathy and compassion? Can I find ways to reassure myself? Can I find people to help me? Are there things I can do, or is there a plan I can make?

8. If the thing I am worrying about actually happened, what steps could I take to address the worry? Working through the situations in your mind will help you realize you don't need to be afraid and help you understand you could handle the situation if it happened.

Let me give you an example. This is a very simple situation, but the questions work very well when applied to more difficult, serious worries and burdens as well.

Situation: "If I have to get up and speak in front of my peers, they will see how frightened I am and think I am a loser. I will be shaking so badly that I will probably drop my papers and lose my place. I am going to end up making a fool of myself and will become the brunt of a lot of mean jokes when I am finished."

1. What would happen if I quit devoting my thoughts and my energy to what could go wrong and spent that energy preparing for a great presentation?

2. Can I really read people's minds? How do I know they will be thinking I am a loser? They might just be feeling grateful that they are not the ones having to speak in front of everyone. Or maybe they will be thinking how

nice I look, or what a good message I am delivering. I cannot read their minds.

3. I am exaggerating. This is just one presentation to a group of friendly faces.

4. Chances are very slim that I will shake so bad that I will drop my papers. In fact, I have actually never seen that happen before.

5. Everything will probably go just fine. I might stumble on a few words, but it is highly unlikely that anything major will happen.

6. I have read stories of great speakers who failed miserably in their first attempts to make speeches, and they didn't let it get them down. They kept working at developing their skills.

7. I will practice on my own and in front of a few friends, and make sure that I breathe deeply and calmly before I present. I will be ready for this. If I do make mistakes, I will use them as learning tools to improve my next presentation.

8. If I dropped my papers and lost my place, I could make light of the situation through humor. For example, I could say, "It turns out, picturing all of you naked in the audience is scaring me more than it's helping me!" It is more than likely that half the audience is asleep anyway, and a blunder like this will actually help them pay attention and remember the presentation.

Forgiveness

When we are working on getting rid of our emotional baggage, forgiveness will most likely be involved in this process—forgiving others and, quite possibly, forgiving ourselves. Confucius, a Chinese philosopher, said, "To be wronged or robbed is nothing unless you continue to remember it."

Our bitterness and anger often cling to us tenaciously. We continually review past wrongs or mistakes over and over in our minds, and as we do this, they gain more and more power over us, until we have become slaves to our own thoughts. The most harmful damage to our hearts, minds, and souls is usually self-inflicted. We allow ourselves to become so tormented by the offenses of others that we fail to realize that our own unforgiving thoughts and attitudes are in reality far more dangerous to our lives than the actual offenses committed against us in the first place.

Forgiveness might sound easy, but in fact it can be one of the most difficult processes to work through. So how do we go about it?

1. Acknowledge the pain and hurt you are experiencing and where it has come from.

2. Decide to use the pain to create a better life for yourself.

3. Understand that you are not excusing the behavior or giving permission for it to be enacted again.

4. Recognize that you and your loved ones are the ones paying the price for an unforgiving heart.

5. Don't dwell on trying to understand "why" it happened. There are things that we will never find answers to, and we must accept this and move on.

6. Take the steps necessary to work through the pain and hurt—pray, meditate, keep a journal, seek professional help—whatever it takes.

7. Let go and move on. Free your thoughts, your mind, your heart, and your soul.

Regret

Regret seems to be a burden that everyone faces. I don't know if there is such a thing as a life without regrets, and I know that if I allowed myself, I could be completely overcome with the regrets of my own life. It seems that at particularly happy times in my life, old thoughts will arise that will remind me of past regrets, and I begin to question my right to happiness. Nothing, however, could be further from the truth, and we need to find ways to overcome these regrets and move forward in life. Here are several suggestions:

1. As with so many burdens in life, you should first acknowledge and then seek to understand your regrets completely and specifically. Record this in your own words, being as specific about the regret as possible.

2. Take full responsibility for your part in the situation.

3. Forgive yourself. As mentioned in the previous section, often forgiving ourselves is the most difficult. If apologizing and making amends is required, do it. Don't put it off and prolong the guilt.

4. Look for the positive in the situation. As difficult as it may be, remember that pain and regret are powerful teachers, and some of our most profound lessons in life are learned in the midst of sorrow and agony.

5. When you have found the lesson, seek to truly understand and accept it. Then when you start to dwell on past mistakes and regrets, refocus your thoughts on the life lessons that have come from the situation.

6. Realize that all lives have regrets. Often we look around and feel that no one could have made the mistakes we have and caused the pain our words or actions have. But the reality is, you are not alone. Seek support in the stories and victories of others.

7. If necessary, seek professional help and support to deal with the emotions associated with the regret, or to plan ways to avoid creating or inviting more events that will leave you with regrets.

Two years ago I seriously damaged the sesmoid bones in my right foot—a repetitive use injury—and ended up in a cast for three months. I had been in pain for many months, but I continued to run on my foot, assuming that it would just heal on its own. I knew better. When the cast came off, the doctor warned me to take it easy on my foot for at least six months. One month later I was approached to play slow-pitch, and instead of allowing my body the proper time to heal, I agreed. During the playoffs we had a double header and had only enough players that night to play the game. In the last inning of the first game I was rounding third base when I caught the corner of the base and severely twisted my ankle. I actually thought that I had broken my ankle because I had absolutely no support to stand. But because we would have to forfeit the second game if I didn't play, I just taped it very tightly and limped through the second game.

By the time I arrived home that night I couldn't move. I pulled in the garage and just honked the horn until my husband came and carried me into the house. I thought I would pass out from the pain. To make a long story short, I had torn all the ligaments in my ankle. Because I had not allowed myself to heal from the previous injury, my ankle had been unstable and susceptible to injury, and this time I was on crutches and then a brace, and I was out of commission for even longer. I learned my lesson the hard way, but I did learn the lesson.

We seem to understand that our bodies need time to heal physically—we wear casts or braces, we use crutches or wheelchairs. But do we allow ourselves time and care to heal emotionally? When we have been hurt emotionally either through trauma, emotional abuse, or doses of constant negativity, disappointment, or discouragement, do we look at ourselves in the same way we would if we were suffering physically? Just think of all the casts and crutches we would see on ourselves, our friends, and our colleagues if our emotional injuries received the same treatment as our physical injuries. We need to address and deal with our emotional injuries and allow them the necessary time to heal.

Strategy #1

Throughout the book we will be using 3-3-3 Strategies, and here is the first one.

Take a few minutes and jot down three "lightweight" items you have in your life suitcase. Celebrate them! Then jot down three burdensome items that are weighing you down. List three steps you can take to lighten your load.

Lightweight Items (Hooray!)

1.

2.

3.

Heavy Items

1.

2.

3.

Three Steps toward Lightening My Load

1.

2.

3.

Chapter 3: Develop Mutually Supportive Relationships

Some people come into our lives and quickly go. Some move our souls to dance. They awaken us to new understanding with the passing whisper of their wisdom and make the sky more beautiful to gaze upon. Some stay for a while and leave footprints on our hearts, and we are never the same.

—Anonymous

In an overscheduled and frantic life, looking after your emotional balance can be a challenge. When I speak about emotional balance, I am not referring to keeping emotions in check, showing no fear, expressing no feeling. A common myth in our society asserts that to be successful one must be tough and invulnerable. In fact, I define emotional balance as making the time to develop and cultivate successful, fulfilling relationships where we can find a place of security to express our emotions, our fears, and our vulnerabilities, and to truly be ourselves. These relationships provide a shelter from the stresses of the world; they provide a place where creativity can flourish and a place where gratitude and hope are carefully nourished.

Developing mutually supportive relationships and friendships is a time consuming job that we often set aside to address more demanding tasks at work. We live in such a fast-paced society that our time for friendships and relationships seems sadly depleted. I was raised in a small community where people dropped by your house unannounced, chatted on street corners, and met up in the local coffee shop to swap stories. Now my life is beyond busy. It seems now that if people wanted to visit me, they would have to book an appointment—probably weeks in advance—to find me actually at home. And instead of relaxing and enjoying a good visit I would probably be frantically checking the clock and worrying about all the things I should be doing. Relationships take time and commitment, and if we want quality relationships in our lives we must dedicate quality time to enhancing them. We need to remember that developing and cultivating a social support network is essential for a healthy mind and body.

My mom died of cancer. Her death had a profound impact on my life, and I will be referring to several life-changing lessons I learned through her death. She was a woman full of love and life. My family and I had the opportunity of caring for her in her own home so she wouldn't have to die in a hospital. We learned incredible lessons from her journey with cancer, with one of the most powerful coming in a rather unexpected tender moment. In the last two weeks of my mom's life she was so heavily medicated for the pain that she would have periods where she felt like the room and her bed were spinning out of control. As desperately as I wanted to, I could not take away her suffering. The only thing I could do for her was take her by the hand and say, over and over, "Mom, I am here. I am right here beside you. I love you. Everything is going to be okay." And that would calm her right down. I think that experience is so relevant to our lives. All of us have times when we feel like our lives are spinning out of control, and we just need someone literally or figuratively to take us by the hand and reassure us that they love us, that they are right beside us, and that everything will be okay.

I love Sheri Dew's story of the little girl who was afraid of the dark—really afraid of the dark. Even when she was old enough to attend grade school, nighttime terrified her. Every night, she and her mother went through the same ritual designed to make her feel secure in her room. But, inevitably, during the night, the girl would sneak into her parents' room and climb in bed with them, at which point her mother would carry her back to her room. Over a period of time, her mother used every argument and tactic she could think of to wean her daughter from the fear of sleeping all night in her own room. Often she would say something to this effect: "Honey, this is your room. You're safe here. Your father and I are just down the hall." And then she would usually add, "God is watching over you. You'll be just fine." One night after this cycle had continually repeated itself, the mother took her daughter back to her room, reassuring her once again, "Honey, you'll be okay. God is watching over you." To which the little girl—who had obviously thought about this—instantly responded, "Mom, don't you know? Sometimes you just need someone with skin on."

It's true. Although our hopes, our dreams, and our faith are essential in our lives, sometimes we just need to hug someone, reach out to someone, or have someone reach out to us. We must not underestimate the importance of our relationships with others, the importance of touching those we come in contact with—both physically and emotionally. Sometimes we just need someone with skin on!

This has always been a difficult area for me to cultivate. I love my children and have incredibly strong ties with my family, but forming "general" relationships is difficult for me. I am somewhat of a hermit by nature. I love my alone time and don't find much comfort in meeting new people or socializing. Let me give you an example. Last summer I flew into a city, presented in front of five hundred people, and then headed back to the airport. No problem, no worries, no big deal. While I was at the airport waiting for my plane to depart, a woman who was in the group to whom I had presented recognized me and came and sat beside me. She was a wonderful woman, and we had a fascinating conversation. We talked for an hour before her plane left, and at the end of that time I was absolutely exhausted. I had a headache, I was edgy, and I felt as if I had run a marathon. Isn't that funny? The five hundred people had been no problem at all, but one on one just about did me in! Yes . . . I am definitely a woman who needs to work on her relationship skills!

Family Relationships

When former First Lady Barbara Bush addressed the graduating students at Wellesley College, she counseled: "As important as your obligations as a doctor, lawyer, or business leader will be, you are a human being first, and those human connections—with your spouses, with children, with friends—are the most important investments you will ever make. At the end of your life, you will never regret not having passed one more test, not winning one more verdict, or not closing one more deal. You will regret time not spent with a husband, a child, a friend, or a parent. . . . Our success as a society depends not on what happens in the White House but on what happens inside your own house."

One of my greatest concerns about our current society is the breakdown of the family. The relationships we form and the work that we do in our families is the most crucial work we can be engaged in. This can be the most difficult work we do because within our family relationships we are the most vulnerable. At home we can be our true selves—we should be safe to explore and overcome weaknesses and insecurities, and to experience unconditional love and acceptance as we strive to find ourselves and become what we would like to be. Home is a place where we can feel a sense of belonging, where we can feel secure and loved, even when we are at our worst. If we do not have strong and supportive family relationships, we lose a crucial place for personal growth and emotional development. Cultivating these relationships can be very rewarding and beneficial. When a family functions effectively, no other influence can have as great an impact on our future success, happiness, and stability.

Of course we realize that not all families function as they should. If your family relationships have been damaged due to dysfunction, remember it is never too late to start the healing process. Perhaps the healing process involves starting fresh—creating your own family and finding the strength and the support to break the cycles of abuse, addiction, or neglect. Whatever the journey, or whatever is necessary, families are worth fighting for.

Toxic Relationships

A careful word of caution with relationships: Choose the people you surround yourself with wisely. Choose positive, optimistic, goal-oriented, supportive friends. Avoid toxic people—you know the type. These are the people who bring you down after only minutes with them. If you ever feel good about life, they will straighten out your thinking very quickly and remind you that there is really very little in life to feel good about. Avoid what I like to call "watercooler workshops." You know the drill. Everyone at work gathers around to discuss the woes of the workplace, and by the time you separate, you are set up to have a discouraging day. The negativity of coworkers can take you away from your own dreams and passions and drag you down into workplace gossip and backbiting.

Strategy #2

1. List the people with whom you spend the most time. Rank them on a scale from 0 to 10 on how supportive and inspirational they are, with 10 being the most supportive and inspirational.

2. Analyze your associates. Have you chosen your relationships well?

3. If you find most of your relationships are negative, perhaps you need to reevaluate the people with whom you associate. And if your toxic associations happen to be with colleagues, your family, or even your spouse— people you may not be in a position to disassociate from your life—make sure you put in place other relationships that counterbalance the negativity, and remember that a positive attitude can be contagious. And even though it may take years, they can eventually come around. Be willing to pay the price to have great relationships in your life.

Chapter 4:
I Am Grateful For . . .

Gratitude unlocks the fullness of life. It turns what we have into enough, and more. It turns denial into acceptance, chaos into order, confusion into clarity. . . . It turns problems into gifts, failures into success, the unexpected into perfect timing, and mistakes into important events. Gratitude makes sense of our past, brings peace for today, and creates a vision for tomorrow.

—Melodie Beattie

Gratitude is one of the most powerful, easily available, yet underused tools to help us find peace and acceptance in our lives. By keeping our focus on what we are grateful for in our lives—instead of focusing on what we don't have or what is wrong—we transform our focus, our thoughts, our vision into something of value, something positive, something forward-moving. Gratitude literally transforms us into better people. When we truly experience and express gratitude, we feel more humility, as opposed to feeling prideful and a sense of entitlement. When we appreciate things we are more respectful and courteous. When our focus is on the good things we have, we are kinder, gentler, and more sensitive to the needs of others. We need to search our lives for the lessons in gratitude that have touched us. I have had many, but there are three of particular influence that I want to share with you.

Lesson Number 1: Find Gratitude in All Things

As my mother was battling cancer, she would awaken each morning with a desire to face the day in the best way that she could, striving to stay busy and active. She was every inch an industrious farm wife and regretted any time that she had to spend lying down or recuperating from the illness that was sapping her strength and forcing her to slow down her normal whirlwind of activity.

With each setback, I saw her regroup and then move forward with a new resolve. The home that she lived in became her source of comfort. My mom and dad lived at their home on the farm their entire married life—she loved her home. There was very little of any monetary worth in her home, but the walls and shelves were filled with gifts and memories from children and grandchildren. If you had ever given anything to mom, no matter how insignificant, you could find it very proudly displayed somewhere in her home.

I learned from her to love these simple things. Even as the cancer ravaged her frail body, I remember the simple pleasures she came to enjoy: family, reading the scriptures, frost, warm hospital blankets, a grandchild's visit, peacocks that roamed the farm, the hymns, a pig in the garden, a phone call, fresh rolls, a good book, polar fleece socks, grocery shopping, sales fliers, and hair. Through this show of quiet gratitude, my mom taught me to have gratitude in my heart always and to express thanks.

She told me over and over again, "I am so blessed," and she expressed heartfelt gratitude to everyone involved with her, from health care workers to friends and family. Every night when I put her to bed she would say, "I'm so glad you are here; I am so blessed with such a wonderful family." Never during this difficult journey did she express anything but gratitude for her life and her family, even though circumstances often seemed unfair and unbearable.

Lesson Number 2: Be Grateful for What You Have

A number of years ago I had a life-changing lesson in gratitude. I was feeling frustrated with the behavior of my thirteen-year-old son. I had a friend who was older and much wiser than I was who sensed my frustration, and I explained the situation to her. I expressed that I just wanted to go home and throttle this teenage son of mine. She very quietly and gently suggested that I should go home and hug him and express my love for him.

You see, several months earlier her twenty-one-year-old son had taken his own life, and of course that act had devastated my friend and her family. I was completely humbled by her suggestion. What heartfelt advice for me.

How many conflicts and how many hurtful words could be avoided if we stepped back, took perspective of the situation, and acknowledged gratitude for what we have rather than frustration for what we feel was missing. How dare I be so ungrateful for the precious gift my son is to me? I did exactly what she suggested, and I tried to think of that experience when the challenge of having teenage children seemed a little too much to bear.

Lesson Number 3: Express Gratitude Daily

My most recent experience with gratitude came a few years later. My mother and father died just several months apart. As I mentioned earlier, my mom died of cancer, and my father was struggling with Alzheimer's at the time of his death. Both of these diseases take heavy tolls on the caregivers. I was emotionally and physically exhausted from the experience.

Shortly after their deaths, my son moved away to college, and then my daughter moved twenty-one hours from home to attend university. I was dealing with a great deal of loss in a very short period of time. At a particularly frustrating time in my daughter's first year away, we established a ritual of emailing each other every morning and ending the email by expressing what we were grateful for that day. We ended with the line "I am grateful for . . ."

This started as a tool to help my daughter, but the benefits on a personal level have been monumental. It is amazing how that simple ritual has transformed our lives and strengthened our relationship. On difficult days we have found that no matter how bad the day might be going, there are always many things that are going right and many things for which to be grateful. It is interesting that our moods can be instantly transformed by listing our blessings in an expression of gratitude.

Learn to Be Genuinely Grateful

If we are feeling discouraged, it is because we have forgotten or suppressed all the reasons we could be feeling happy. And, conversely, if we are feeling good, it is because we are not dwelling on all the reasons we could be feeling discouraged. It's just that simple. We need to incorporate genuine gratitude into our lives. When the alarm rings in the morning, instead of cursing and starting a dialogue of negativity about how early it is and how we wish we didn't have to go to work, we could just say "thank you." We need to be grateful for the day and the many opportunities we will be able to create through our gratitude and happiness.

If this is a difficult concept for you, take it seriously and learn to become genuinely grateful. Keep a record of your gratitude by carrying a recipe card or notepad and writing down all the things you encounter that you can be grateful for in the day. Don't go to bed until you have expressed gratitude for at least ten people or things. You will find that this "attitude of gratitude" will become a part of your thinking and an integral part of your life.

Hope goes hand in hand with gratitude. While carrying out research for my master's degree, I became fascinated with the topic of hope. It was a few months prior to my returning to university that I had watched my mom wage her eighteen-month battle against ovarian cancer, and I saw the difference both physically and emotionally that her unwavering hope and faith made in the quality of her life during this difficult time. I soon became a firm believer in the importance of hope in our lives. Margaret Sommerville put it beautifully by saying, "Hope is the oxygen of the human spirit," (quoted in P. J. Frost's *Toxic Emotions at Work*).

Like gratitude, hope is a highly undervalued tool that can lead us to success and happiness in our lives. Researchers are finding that hope is much more than wishful thinking that can give us comfort in difficult times. It is actually a powerful predictor of success in all areas of our lives—hopeful students do better in their school performance, hopeful athletes achieve more success in their competitions, hopeful salesmen increase their sales, to name a few. We must have hope!

My daughter loves orchids. Recently we took a cruise around the Hawaiian Islands. On the island of Hawaii, we were able to visit the

Mauna Loa volcano—the earth's largest volcano and one of the most active volcanoes on earth. We were fascinated with a particular type of orchid called the bromeliad, which, in the midst of the devastation caused by the lava rock, had found a way for its roots to penetrate the cracks and fissures and locate moisture and organic nutrients. We were told this particular species can also be found growing on sheer cliff faces, while another species of bromeliad can be found growing on telephone poles or even on the telephone lines themselves. Now that is hope! That is never giving up in the face of adversity. That is finding a way!

That is what gratitude and hope are all about. Even in the midst of adversity, you can look for those cracks and fissures, look beyond the impossibility of the situation and find the good, find the positive, find a way!

Strategy #3

Design an expression of daily gratitude in your life.

or

Start a gratitude journal: Every day for three weeks, write three things you are grateful for and three positive things that happened during the day.

For fascinating information on the research of hope and optimism, read Martin Seligman's *Learned Optimism.*

Chapter 5:
The Power of the Mind

No thought lives in your head rent free. . . . You will pay for negative thoughts in energy, time, health, and unhappiness.

—*T. Harv Eker*

There is an incredibly powerful connection between our thoughts, our emotions, and our stress. Several months ago my daughter became frighteningly ill. I immediately flew down to be with her and my son-in-law. I am a stress management consultant. I understand stress, I have strategies to deal with stress, and I can handle stress. Or so I thought. I was sure I had managed to keep myself quite composed and together during the whole ordeal. However, my "state of mind" became quite clear one afternoon when I thought I would walk a short distance to the grocery store to pick up a few things for my daughter. I got to the store and purchased the groceries. I then proceeded to leave and left my purchases sitting at the till. I had to be called back to take my groceries with me. When I got to the busy street corner to cross, I waited patiently for the walk symbol to appear. Five minutes and three light changes later, I finally came to my senses and realized it was time to pay attention and cross the street. Perhaps I wasn't quite as together as I presumed. We have all had similar experiences in which our emotions seemed to take over our brains for a period of time. Daniel Goleman, in his book *Emotional Intelligence*, explains that our strong emotions create "neural static" and disrupt our thinking. So when you feel like you just can't think straight when you are stressed out, you are right.

Much has been written about the power of thought in recent years. Taking the time to analyze your thinking and the incredible influence it has over you can literally change your life. The bottom line is: if you do not change your thinking, you cannot change your life. Interestingly, our thoughts have a profound impact on how stress affects us. Every thought has an emotion attached to it. We are not stressed until we have a stressful thought.

Our thoughts often have a domino effect. Sometimes we start with a thought that when focused on can begin to grow, and then we feel a little stressed. If we continue to focus on that thought, we begin to feel a little angry and a little more stressed, until eventually the thoughts take over our minds and emotions, and it becomes what Richard Carlson calls a full-blown "thought attack." Let's look at a simple example. I think most of us have been in a fender bender with our vehicles. When something happens, we immediately start telling ourselves a story. "Why me? This is the worst thing that could have possibly happened. This is going to cost so much money. My spouse is going to kill me. This will ruin my plans for the day, the week, the month. I am useless when I get behind the wheel." And so on. You know the dance. That kind of thinking immediately triggers more stress, more frustration, and more anxiety. And these feelings often lead to unfortunate actions or behaviors. Perhaps we did not have control over the accident happening, but we do have control over the story we tell ourselves. What if we change our thinking to "I am so lucky I am not hurt. This could have been so much more serious. What would I do without good car insurance? I am grateful the kids were not riding with me. I will have to rearrange my schedule, but everything will be okay." We need to engage in "stress reducing" thinking instead of "stress increasing" thinking.

The idea of a "thought attack" parallels in many ways a heart attack. And, interestingly, there are some helpful comparisons that we can draw between the two—specifically in the area of prevention. The American Heart Association has outlined the ABCs of heart disease prevention. They are to avoid tobacco, be more active, and choose good nutrition. Let's reword those ABCs to help us prevent thought attacks.

Avoid drawing toxic thoughts into your mind. A sure way to bring in toxins is to associate with toxic people.

Be more active with your mind. Learn to love learning. Pursue a hobby. Sign up for an interesting seminar. Take a college course. Learn a new skill. Memorize a poem or motto. Never stop learning and exercising your mind. This leaves little time or space for negative, destructive thinking.

Choose good nutrition for your mind. Read good literature and fill your mind with inspirational stories, empowering thoughts, and motivational knowledge.

Just as the AHA's motto states: "It's not enough to know your risk factors. You've got to take action for your heart." So it is with thoughts. It is not enough to know your risk factors of negative thinking. You have got to be proactive and aware of the power of your mind.

T. Harv Eker, in his book *Secrets of the Millionaire Mind*, tells us that "training and managing your own mind is the most important skill you could ever own, in terms of both happiness and success." The most powerful tool we can bring on board to enhance our lives and our happiness is our minds. Research indicates that the average person talks to himself or herself about fifty thousand times per day. Most of that self-talk is about yourself, and 80 percent of it is negative. So really, during almost every moment of every day you are thinking or talking yourself either into or out of success. Every thought matters. Every thought is bringing you serenity, inspiration, or stress. Every thought is taking you to your desired destination or moving you further away. No thoughts are neutral; our minds and particularly our thoughts have a profound impact on how stress affects us. The way we perceive a situation triggers the stress response, so we are not stressed until we think stressful thoughts. Our thought processes, whether positive or negative, optimistic or pessimistic, determine our levels of stress and ultimately our actions and reactions to what is going on around us.

We need to take the time to do a self-analysis and discover how we think, how we react in different situations, what we tell ourselves, where we allow our thoughts to take us, what values, paradigms, and rules we have in our hearts and minds. If the rules we have in our heads set us up for disappointment and discouragement, perhaps we need to rewrite the rules. For example: if you are setting out on a vacation and the rules you have in your head state that you can only enjoy this vacation if the weather is perfect, the children are well behaved, and nothing goes wrong, then as soon as the wind blows, the rain comes, the children fight, or you have a flat tire, then your vacation is ruined. Maybe you need to change the rules in your head. Just maybe the rule needs to be that regardless of what happens, you will be spending time with your family and making memories.

I want to share a bit of my own journey on this particular topic. This has probably been the most difficult area for me to work on in my goal of achieving balance, but it is without a doubt the most fulfilling and life-changing process I have ever embarked on. I was raised on a farm with five older brothers and sisters. I had an amazing upbringing. Each of my older siblings is my hero and has qualities that I love and admire. My parents loved me unconditionally. They taught me to have faith, to work hard, and to live with integrity. We had a simple, happy life.

In my early twenties I went through a series of devastating events that left me with serious trust issues and a discouraged attitude about life. I became a worrier. I was a single mom of two beautiful children, and I stayed awake at night solving all the world's problems. I then spent most of the day being tired and discouraged in my work, and hoping and dreaming of the day I would retire with my pension. I was also a great pretender. I'm sure people who know me very well will be surprised when they read this. I was able to fake happiness and enthusiasm better than any other person I know. I pretended to love my work, while everyday I deeply resented not being able to stay home and be a mom. I felt guilty and bitter that I had been deprived of the one thing I had aspired to my whole life. I was a working mom and raced from one commitment to another—never considering that I could say no to anything or slow down for a minute and actually take care of my own needs so that I would be better prepared to love and serve my family.

I really can't pinpoint the turning point in my life. I see it as a journey taken one step at a time with many influences along the way. In my late thirties I started to question whether I was brave enough to make some changes in my life and explore new career choices. I started to question my beliefs about success and started dreaming of all the ways I could help people and enjoy my family if I allowed myself to dream that there was something more out there for me. My entire way of thinking was starting to change. I started to change the way I spoke to myself. This process did not happen overnight—in fact it is still a journey and will continue to be a journey for the rest of my life. But now it is a journey of opportunities, dreams, goals, successes, failures, and learning . . . so much learning! My nights are filled with positive affirmations and visualizing successes, instead of anticipating the next thing that could possibly go wrong and dwelling on past mistakes and injustices.

In fact, an interesting thing happened several months ago. Once again I experienced a serious trauma—an experience where my self-dignity had been completely degraded. I was humiliated and devastated, and old feelings of unworthiness and defeat started to creep back into my life. But the interesting thing was that those old feelings of negativity now felt uncomfortable to me—they were no longer my comfort zone for discouragement and self-pity. I was unable to stay in that state for long. My newly developed thought patterns would not allow me to revert back. They were strong enough to pull me out of my misery and get me back on track. And that is what I want for you . . . for everyone. Life has extremely difficult challenges to face, there is no doubt about it. But we can be happy on the journey! We don't need to understand all our challenges, we just need to have faith that they happen for a reason in a big picture that we don't have a clear vision of yet.

So my plea for you is to start today to change or expand your thinking.

Strategy #4

Set a goal today to change what is going on in your mind. Be specific. Be consistent. Be constantly vigilant. This is NOT a "think happy thoughts" solution. These need to be changes in thought patterns that permeate your very being. Take three recipe cards (or as many as necessary) and write down three positive statements about what you want your life to be. Make the statements in the present tense, and have them fill your mind. Find three times a day for three weeks to conscientiously think these thoughts, and whenever you have down time and negative thoughts start to creep in replace them with your new thoughts. Use a schedule and make yourself accountable for doing this.

Joanne Steed-Takasaki with Jayme Pierringer

Let me share some of my positive statements:

I have incredible energy and focus in achieving_____.

I am living in wellness and prosperity, and serving God in humility.

Money flows easily into my life from many different sources.

I have absolute certainty I can accomplish_____.

Thought Reconditioning Schedule

I use a weekly schedule like the one shown below to ensure that three times every day I repeat my positive mantra and then put a check mark under each day. This keeps me accountable for positive thinking.

Monday	Tuesday	Wednesday	Thursday	Friday	Saturday	Sunday

Chapter 6: Exercise Education

*Any type of discipline requires breaking
through the pain—short-term pain in
order to gain long-term pleasure.*

—Anthony Robbins

As previously noted, I am passionate about working in the fitness industry. I find fulfillment in guiding the transformation of people's minds and bodies as they incorporate regular physical activity into their stressful, overbooked lives. A fitness center is like my own "stress lab." I see patrons come in with the weight and stress of work and life written in their faces and carried in their bodies, but they leave with a lifted weight and a renewed focus and energy to carry on.

The numerous benefits of regular exercise vary from person to person. Of course the health benefits are universal—lowering your risk of heart attack, strengthening your bones, and decreasing your risk of diabetes are among the most important. However, patrons I speak to mention things like increasing self-esteem, increasing strength, feeling healthier, sleeping better, controlling weight, looking good, reducing stress, providing time for self, and improving attitude and outlook as their personal rewards for taking the time to exercise.

It is important to realize that making time to exercise does not need to involve working out in an intimidating gym environment with a bunch of muscle heads. (Although a personal trainer can give you the knowledge to turn that intimidating gym into your playground.) Participating in recreational sports, walking the dog, jogging, parking farther away, and using the stairs can all be great ways to get you off the couch and on your way to physical fitness.

The psychological benefits of exercise result from the release of chemical substances during your workout. The brain neurotransmitters called endorphins that are secreted by the brain during exercise decrease pain and produce feelings of well-being. The brain chemical dopamine, which is important for motivation, incentive, and energy, is also secreted during exercise. In addition, when you are about to exercise, the hormones epinephrine and norepinephrine are released and begin to prepare your body for physical activity. After your workout is finished the parasympathetic nervous system signals the secretions of these chemicals to stop, and a calming sensation results allowing your body to return to homeostasis or its usual resting state. The more fit you are, the quicker this rebound effect happens in the body. This is called a "parasympathetic rebound" and is one of the reasons that exercise can be such an effective stress management tool.

Research also tells us that physical fitness and exercise can increase cognitive function. Moderate- to high-intensity exercise increases the flow of blood to the brain, supplying oxygen and glucose to enhance brain function. So if you want to get smarter, exercise!

Don't be overwhelmed by the idea of starting a fitness program—or just turn off as soon as the word *exercise* is mentioned. Start small and basic and go from there.

Step 1: Begin by doing something every day to increase your physical activity as a part of your daily routine.

Step 2: Start walking, or doing any other low-impact activity, to build your endurance.

Step 3: Exercise at the right intensity and duration for your age and health. Find a more structured program.

Step 4: Start playing sports, set a goal to run a 10K, try different cross-training techniques.

If you choose to join a gym, join with a friend, or hire a personal trainer immediately so that you don't need to feel lost or intimidated in the gym environment. Set short- and long-term goals—try new programs, new equipment, new classes. Do whatever it takes to stay committed. If you can stay committed long enough to see results, what you see and feel can be highly motivational. Understanding the benefits of exercise, finding something that you enjoy, finding something that is quite convenient, and having a support system are all important factors in being able to stick with an exercise regime.

When I ask our regular gym patrons what keeps them coming, I hear things like "I feel guilty if I don't come," "I can't cope with stress as well when I don't come," "It's just a part of my life now," and "I'm addicted." Create the mindset that you are a "gym rat," a "soccer player," a "fitness fanatic," or a "runner" and then fulfill that mindset.

When exercising, keep these three principles in mind: frequency, intensity, and duration. In other words, **moderate** physical activity for **30–45 minutes per day** will provide significant health benefits to your life. Remember to warm up before exercising and to cool down and stretch following exercise. Your warm-up increases blood flow to the muscles so they stretch easily, reducing the risk of muscle tears. It also elevates your core body temperature, lubricates your joints, and carries oxygen to your heart. The cool-down gradually decreases your level of activity. Your cool-down period prevents blood from pooling in your muscles without returning to the heart. Without a proper cool-down you may become dizzy or nauseated. Stretching, another essential part of the workout, builds flexibility and develops range of motion. Use gentle and fluid motions, breathe deeply, and maintain each stretch for at least twenty seconds. Also, stay properly hydrated during your workout.

Strategy #5

1. Choose a physical activity you enjoy or think you could enjoy. Choosing the right physical activity is essential. Your choice of activity will depend on what you are interested in, your schedule, your need to be with people or to be alone, and your main goals for exercise.

2. Write your goals down. Remember a goal is just a wish until you write it down. Be specific. Make schedules. Set deadlines. Outline the important benefits and rewards you will receive from exercise. Display your goals where you can see them regularly.

3. Have the courage and commitment to carry out your plan. Make sure you have built in accountability—have a friend go walking with you, join a rec league with your coworkers, have an accountability partner you report to weekly, hire a personal trainer to make you accountable at the gym.

A very basic sample jogging program appears below. You can see the pattern and continue progressing at your desired rate. Try to incorporate at least three days a week into your program. Start each session with ten minutes of dynamic stretching. Dynamic stretching uses active muscular effort to bring about a stretch. Walking lunges, arm circles, walking high knee grabs, and exaggerated kicks would be examples of dynamic stretching movements.

Week Number	Activity	Cool-down	Total Time
1	Walk nonstop 10 minutes	Walk slowly 3 minutes; stretch 2 minutes	15 minutes
2	Walk 5 minutes; jog 1 minute; walk 5 minutes; jog 1 minute	Walk slowly 3 minutes; stretch 2 minutes	17 minutes
3	Walk 5 minutes; jog 2 minutes; walk 5 minutes; jog 2 minutes	Walk slowly 3 minutes; stretch 2 minutes	19 minutes
4	Walk 5 minutes; jog 3 minutes; walk 5 minutes; jog 3 minutes	Walk slowly 3 minutes; stretch 2 minutes	21 minutes
5	Walk 5 minutes; jog 4 minutes; walk 5 minutes; jog 4 minutes	Walk slowly 3 minutes; stretch 2 minutes	23 minutes
6	Walk 4 minutes; jog 5 minutes; walk 4 minutes; jog 5 minutes	Walk slowly 3 minutes; stretch 2 minutes	23 minutes
7	Walk 4 minutes; jog 6 minutes; walk 4 minutes; jog 6 minutes	Walk slowly 3 minutes; stretch 2 minutes	25 minutes
8	Walk 4 minutes; jog 7 minutes; walk 4 minutes; jog 7 minutes	Walk slowly 3 minutes; stretch 2 minutes	27 minutes

9	Walk 4 minutes; jog 8 minutes; walk 4 minutes; jog 8 minutes	Walk slowly 3 minutes; stretch 2 minutes	29 minutes
10	Walk 4 minutes; jog 9 minutes; walk 4 minutes; jog 9 minutes	Walk slowly 3 minutes; stretch 2 minutes	31 minutes
11	Walk 4 minutes; jog 15 minutes	Walk slowly 3 minutes; stretch 2 minutes	24 minutes
12	Walk 4 minutes; jog 20 minutes	Walk slowly 3 minutes; stretch 2 minutes	29 minutes

Basic Fitness Program

Program Components:
Warm-up: 5–10 minutes
Cardio: 20–45 minutes
Weights
Abdominals
Stretching

Monday	Tuesday	Wednesday	Thursday	Friday	Saturday	Sunday
Cardio Weights Abs Stretch	Cardio Stretch*	Cardio Weights Abs Stretch	Cardio Stretch	Cardio Weights Abs Stretch		

*Do not lift weights on consecutive days unless using a split program.

Body Part	Exercise	Reps	Sets	Weight	Notes
Back:	Seated Row	10	2–3		
	Lat Pulldown	10	2–3		
Chest:	Chest Press	10	2–3		
Shoulders:	Shoulder Press	10	2–3		

Arms:	Bicep Curls	10	2–3		
	Tricep Rope Pressdown	10	2–3		
Legs:	Leg Press	10	2–3		
	Lunges				
	1/2 squats with a BOSU				
Abdominals:	Bridge Dips				
	Fitball Side to Side				
	Fitball Crunch				
Stretches:	Hamstring				

	Quad				
	Glut				
	Tricep				
	Bicep and Shoulder				
	Back				

Clip art provided by www.trainerclipart.com.

Chapter 7: Nutrition in a Nutshell

The moment you want a goal more than you want an excuse, you can succeed.

—*Tommy Newberry*

We live in an age and a society where we now recognize that poor eating habits and a lack of nutritional knowledge can contribute to obesity, disease, poor fitness, and low energy. We understand that it is necessary to start making correct food choices and living healthier lifestyles.

In principle, eating well is not a difficult concept. It involves eating a selection of foods that supply the appropriate amount of essential nutrients and energy to sustain us in our lives. However, there are numerous factors that influence our eating patterns and often make the task of eating seem complicated and overwhelming.

So why is it so difficult to make wise food choices? The foods that taste the best to us are often sweet and salty. We eat when we gather socially, and social pressure often influences us to make choices to eat when we are not hungry or to eat bad foods when we are trying to eat more wisely. Three other powerful factors are the availability, the convenience, and the affordability of so many foods. Obviously you don't eat as much if food is not easily available and affordable. And many of us cope with stress, loneliness, boredom, and anxiety with food. With so many factors to consider, how do we even begin to clean up our eating habits?

These nutrition recommendations are quite simple:

- Try not to let yourself get too hungry. Hunger depletes the energy you need to make wise food choices. Instead of eating two or three large meals, eat five or six small meals a day. By eating smaller meals and eating more frequently, you can keep your blood sugar more regulated.

- Don't participate in fad diets—make a lifestyle change instead.

- Eat a balanced diet with a variety of foods that will provide you with the six basic nutrients for health: carbohydrates, fat, protein, vitamins, minerals, and water. Following the Canada Food Guide or the USDA Food Pyramid will get you on the right path.

- Go natural. When possible, make natural choices—choose a baked potato instead of French fries, or an orange instead of orange juice.

- Don't deprive yourself. Just use wisdom and moderation in your choice of "junk food" options.

- Don't skip breakfast. If you feel you don't have enough time, prepare a healthy on-the-go breakfast the night before. Peanut butter sandwiches and juice boxes, yogurt, a piece of fruit, muffins, or blender drinks can all be easily transported with you. If you are not hungry at breakfast time, carefully evaluate what you are eating the night before. Late-night snacking can definitely influence your morning appetite.

- Quit eating two hours before bedtime.

- Take the time to enjoy every bite of food instead of wolfing it down mindlessly.

If you are concerned about achieving or maintaining a healthy weight, keep in mind that the recommended maximal weight loss per week is two pounds. Calorie counting can be helpful in the early stage of lifestyle changes, but remember that eventually the best idea is to forget calories and just think about eating healthy. There are 3,500 calories in a pound of body fat, so a deficit of 7,000 calories per week, or 1,000 calories per day, would be necessary for the optimal loss of two pounds per week. This can be created through limiting food intake or through exercise or through a combination of both. Use the following chart to help you calculate your approximate daily caloric intake needed to maintain a desirable body weight.

Activity level	Calories per pound	Calories per kilogram
Very sedentary	13	29
Sedentary	14	31
Moderate activity	15	33
Very active	16	38
Competitive athlete	17+	38+

For example: If I presently weigh 150 lbs. and lead a sedentary lifestyle, I will take 14 x 150 = 2,100. I will require 2,100 calories per day to maintain my present weight. If I wish to embark on a weight loss program, I want to create a deficit in that number either through food intake or exercise or both. Keep in mind when working to achieve a healthy weight, or in making a healthy lifestyle change, that success breeds success. So in any endeavor it is important to set short-term, attainable goals so you can achieve multiple successes on your journey toward your long-term goal.

Keeping a record of your activity and eating patterns can help you closely examine the behaviors that might be holding you back. Sometimes we don't realize our habits or behavior patterns until we track them by writing them down and analyzing them. Fill out the following log with all your food consumption and activities for a two-week period and then ask yourself the following questions:

1. At what times of the day are you eating?

2. How much are you eating?

3. What seems to be triggering your eating? Is it hunger? Stress? Boredom? Habit?

4. How active are you?

5. At what times of the day are you most active?

6. How are you feeling during these activities?

These questions will give you feedback on your motivation for eating, the kinds of food choices you are making, the times of day you are most likely to enjoy being active, and ultimately the lifestyle changes you need to make.

Now is the time to decide . . . are you going to get a new belt or a new lifestyle?

Time of day	Activity	Location	Food	Amount eaten	Hunger level	Feelings/ emotions
Sample: 7 p.m.	Watching TV	Bedroom	Pop/ potato chips	1 can 1 bag	Low	Bored

There are a number of good websites that can be very helpful in tracking your eating habits and outlining your nutritional intake. Check out www.fitday.com or www.caloriecount.com.

Chapter 8:
Making Time to Relax

All glory comes from daring to begin.

—*Eugene F. Ware*

We live in a society today in which "busy" is the norm. We wear our "busyness" like a badge of honor and take great pride in how tight our schedules are. But at what cost? Our families, our bodies, our minds all pay a price. One of my dear friends shared with me that her daughter's first sentence was "Hurry up kids! We are going to be late!"

Words like *relaxation* and *meditation* have become foreign to our minds and our lives. But the reality is that taking twenty to thirty minutes out of your day to train your body and mind to relax will decrease your anxiety, lower your blood pressure, lower tension and pain in your muscles, and improve your general feelings of well being. Let's examine some simple methods of relaxation to build into your day.

Music

Music can have a huge impact on your emotional state. In his book *The Mozart Effect*, Don Campbell outlines numerous studies with conclusions that indicate certain types of music can enhance learning and heal the body. To name a few of these positive effects, music influences the relaxation process by slowing down and equalizing brain waves, by affecting the heartbeat, pulse rate, and blood pressure, by reducing muscle tension and improving body movement and coordination, by increasing endorphins, by regulating stress-related hormones, by boosting immune function, by stimulating digestion, and by generating a sense of safety and well-being.

It is important when using music as a relaxation technique that your choice of music be appropriate. Music for the purpose of relaxation must be peaceful and soothing. It is important to remember that music can negatively stimulate as well as relax, depending on the type of music you choose. Classical music, in particular Mozart and his contemporaries, will have the soothing effects you seek. Sounds like the tide, birds chirping, and breezes blowing can also facilitate relaxation.

Breathing

It is no secret that breathing is an essential process of life. Of course we could not live without it. Simply put, breathing allows us to transport oxygen from the air to every cell in our bodies. It is also essential in the removal of waste products like carbon dioxide. Our bodies require oxygen in every cell in order to function properly. Even slight changes in the oxygen levels in our brains can alter our feelings or actions. Shallow breathing associated with emotions like fear, anxiety, and anger can actually lower the levels of oxygen in the brain and cause irritability, impulsiveness, and confusion.

We need to train ourselves to breathe properly . . . to breathe deeply. The way we breathe can literally affect how we are feeling every minute of the day. Most of us carry out what is referred to as chest breathing. We breathe from the upper part of our chests—quick, shallow breaths that allow less oxygen into our bodies. Rapid, shallow chest breathing can cause a drop in the body's CO_2 levels, which causes an increase in the blood pH level, causing a constriction of the blood vessels that supply the brain. The reduced blood flow to the brain can cause lightheadedness, heart palpitations, numbness, tingling, weakness, agitation, and shortness of breath. Breathing deeply is a little recognized and not well understood technique to quiet your mind, activate your parasympathetic nervous system, and relax your body and soul. So let's get you tapped into this powerful tool in three easy steps.

Step 1

Analyze how you presently breathe. Place one hand on your abdomen and one on your chest. Take three deep breaths. When you inhale, does the hand on your chest rise more, or do you find the hand on your abdomen moving significantly? If the hand on your chest is rising, you are utilizing shallow chest breathing, and if the hand on your abdomen is moving outward as you breathe in, you are using deep, diaphragmatic breathing. The hand on your chest should remain stationary. Our goal is to utilize diaphragmatic breathing easily and consistently. This ensures greater oxygen consumption and greater waste exchange.

Step 2

To become comfortable and familiar with diaphragmatic breathing, lie on your back and place a book on your abdomen. Breathe through your nose. Hold the sides of the book as you inhale. The book should be lifted away from your body as your abdomen expands during inhalation, and during exhalation the book should return toward your body. Once this feels comfortable, replace the book with your hands. Anytime during the day when you want to refocus your breathing or analyze your technique, just place your hands on your abdomen and check to ensure your abdomen is expanding outward during inhalation and being drawn inward during exhalation.

Step 3

Practice. Utilize this technique when you start to feel anxious or stressed. Your body will automatically try to employ shallow chest breathing, so make a conscious effort not to use this method. During times of stress make a conscious shift to deep, steady, diaphragmatic breathing.

Stepping back from a stressful situation and taking three deep breaths can be an instant stress reliever. Use deep breathing before and after any stressful situation.

Yoga

Yoga can be very relaxing and healing. Not only learning the Eastern poses, but also gaining an understanding of the Eastern philosophy can help you make deeper mind/body connections and gain a deeper self-awareness. Yoga enhances your ability to live in the moment. Often your mind is still at work or otherwise preoccupied when it needs to be completely present in whatever activity you are pursuing. Yoga helps you connect to the present—also referred to as mindfulness.

Stress is often caused by a preoccupation with past guilt, regret, and shame, or with a fear of future events. Mindfulness encourages you to focus your attention on the present moment, which makes it an excellent strategy to relieve stress. When you attend a yoga class, you are asked to identify your intention for attending the class.

Yoga helps participants to learn to connect and respond to the messages of their bodies, and to learn to breathe effectively and properly. Yoga also helps participants connect to their emotional bodies and practice acceptance of themselves. According to Eastern philosophy, we judge ourselves even more than we judge others. To accept what is present just as it is helps you to become less judgmental and is the gateway to contentment and happiness. Studies have found yoga increases spatial memory, improves body awareness, decreases resting heart rate, and enhances physical relaxation.

Massage

Research also reveals the enormous benefits of touch. The healing, soothing, relaxing effects of massage are well documented and widely acclaimed in our society today. Massage soothes the mind and body, and it is thought to stimulate the flow of endorphins through the body. Professional massages have been found to enhance immunity by stimulating lymph flow, to improve circulation by pumping oxygen and nutrients into tissues and organs, and to reduce anxiety and stress, as well as providing a number of other benefits.

Self-massage can be an effective stress reducer at the office, on the plane, in the car, during any kind of delays, or anywhere else stress can strike. Some of the same techniques for the partner massage can also be utilized on your own. You can stimulate circulation in your head by making firm, circular movements with your fingertips on your scalp and forehead. To reduce tension in your hands, use your thumb to stroke the opposite hand from the knuckle to the wrist, or squeeze and then gently stretch each finger separately. To calm your nerves, close your eyes and stroke your fingers from the bridge of the nose over the eyebrows to your temples. To relieve pressure in your ears, apply pressure in small circular motions to the front of your ears, just below the jawbone, and then behind your ears. Closing your eyes and stroking one hand after another from the bridge of your nose and up to your hairline will instill deep relaxation, and cupping your hands over your eyes and applying small circular motions to your temples will help relieve headaches.

Learn to listen to your body. When you feel the stress response taking place in your body, take action. Create your own quick fix for stress. With any of the following strategies you should be able to provide some relief in seconds. I call them "Six-Second Stress Stabilizers." Read them over and design your own sequence of stress-relieving steps to calm your mind and body. Be patient. Training yourself to relax takes time and requires frequent reminders. Place sticky notes in frequently visited areas with words like *relax* or *breathe*, or other cue words written on them.

Here are some ideas for Six-Second Stress Stabilizers:

1. Breathe deeply: Take five deep breaths. Make sure you breathe fully and evenly. When you breathe in, think about bringing peace into your mind and body. When you breathe out, think about releasing the stress from your mind and body.
    Breathe in—say in your mind or out loud, "peace."
    Breathe out—say in your mind or out loud, "relax."
    Choose whatever words will work the best for you.

2. Stop thoughts! Replace negative thoughts with positive, stress-reducing thoughts.

3. Squeeze and relax your fists and arms.

4. Place your left hand on your right shoulder by your neck and gently squeeze the flesh between your palms and your fingers. (This is where I carry my stress!) Hold this for several seconds, then release. Work along the shoulder and on top of the arm—wherever it feels tight. Alternate on the left shoulder.

5. Body check: If you have the opportunity to sit in a comfortable chair, do a quick body check. Close your eyes if you are able to, and, starting with your toes, move upward and think about each body part. Ask

yourself where you are feeling tense, and as you come to those tense areas, gently tighten them for a brief period of time and then relax. If you have more time you can go through each body part and consciously tighten and then relax each area of your body. The body check can take place at any time, in any setting, and in any position.

6. Close your eyes and gently massage your temples for sixty seconds.

7. Take your hands and rub your thighs until you can feel the warmth generated in them.

8. Stretch your arms in front, behind your back, or over your head and hold for ten seconds.

9. Listen to calming, soothing music.

Strategy #6

Design your own sequence of Six-Second Stress Stabilizers from this chapter or from other strategies that you have found helpful. Practice using this strategy when you are feeling stressed.

Six-Second Stress Strategies:

1.

2.

3.

Chapter 9: Laughter and Other Great Medicines

Laughter translates into any language.

—Anonymous

When was the last time you observed a group of young children? After years of working in an elementary school, I have had the opportunity of watching children in all kinds of settings. Children laugh a lot. They laugh loudly. They laugh deeply. They laugh spontaneously. They laugh long and hard. They laugh until they can hardly stand. Adults don't. Can you think of the last time you laughed until you could you hardly stand? I can. And to be honest it is one of the few times in my adult life that I remember laughing completely uninhibited—laughing like a child. My family and I attended the Danny Gans comedy act in Las Vegas, and each one of us laughed until we could hardly breathe. We laughed constantly throughout the entire show. We laughed loudly. We laughed deeply. We laughed long and hard. It was an amazing experience, and it was so cathartic. I left feeling more energized and alive than I had felt in a very long time And I left wishing we could experience that feeling more often.

There is a very good reason I felt that way. The effects of laughter on health have been studied for many years. Laughter raises the body temperature, decreases pulse and blood pressure, contracts and relaxes muscles, causes breathing to become deeper, increases oxygen exchange, and increases the production of catecholamines and endorphins. Periods of deep laughter are followed by a state of relaxation, which returns respiration, heart rate, blood pressure, and muscle tension to below-normal levels. Laughter also relieves anxiety, tension, and stress, improves the immune function, increases pain tolerance, and decreases the stress response.

Indiana State University conducted a study on the effects of laughter on natural killer cells. Their findings suggest that laughter may be a useful cognitive-behavioral intervention in people with cancer and HIV disease. Wooten, in the article "Humor: An Antidote to Stress," promotes laughter as an effective self-care tool in coping with stress. Wooten also outlines the research that has been done on the effects that laughter has on the immune function and resilience to stress.

Lee Berk, a professor of pathology and anatomy at Loma Linda University in California, has been studying the health benefits of laughter since the 1980s. In one study, he drew three samples of blood from ten volunteers before they watched a one-hour comedy video. He took more blood samples at ten-minute intervals during the comedy and three more after the show was over. His findings indicate that laughter actually lowers the levels of the primary stress hormone, cortisol. In 2001, Berk performed a study of cardiac patients. He followed the progress of two separate groups of patients for a year after their heart attacks. One group was prescribed thirty minutes of comedy per day, combined with their medical therapy. The other group only received the medical therapy. At the end of the year, the group with the "laughter prescription" had lower blood pressure, lower stress-hormone levels, fewer episodes of arrhythmia, and fewer repeat heart attacks. I'll let you be the judge. Who says laughter isn't great medicine?

Examine your own life. Can you imagine lying awake in bed at night thinking of all the fun you had or all the happiness you experienced in a day? Probably not. Those kinds of experiences don't haunt you and keep you tossing and turning as worry and anxiety do.

"I'm so stressed out," "there is never enough time," "I am too busy to think straight." How often do you hear those responses when you are engaged in a conversation with someone? When was the last time you heard someone complaining about how much fun and laughter they had engaged in that day or how much relaxation they had indulged in?

I've been to a lot of funerals, and not once have I heard a eulogy celebrating how busy a person was, how stressed they were, or how inspired we could be by a person's overscheduled, overburdened life. Rather, eulogies celebrate relationships, happy times, and inspirational accomplishments on a very personal level.

We need to consciously plan more laughter into our lives. Laughter is free, it is contagious, and it provides us with a connection to others—so use it!

Just a quick word of caution. Remember that laughter should never be directed at anyone. We all know that laughter and humor can be used inappropriately to hurt others.

Water and Wellness

When working on achieving balance and wellness in your life, don't forget about water! Water is one of my favorite "de-stressors." Water has been used to stimulate healing for centuries. Approximately two-thirds of our body weight consists of water, and water plays a number of important roles in our bodies. It regulates body temperature; moistens the tissues in the ear, nose, throat, and eyes; helps prevent constipation; carries nutrients and oxygen to the cells; lubricates joints; flushes waste out of the kidneys and liver; and helps dissolve minerals and other nutrients so they can be used by the body.

There are actually no scientific studies to support the "drink eight eight-ounce glasses of water per day" rule, but it is a logical guideline to follow and will typically replace the fluid you lose in a day through breathing, perspiration, and excretion. Alcohol, tea, coffee, and soda are not great choices for satisfying thirst and rehydrating the body, and in some cases they can actually dehydrate instead. Water is calorie-free, cheap, and easily accessible in most parts of the world. Remember, it is generally not a good idea to use thirst as a guideline for drinking. You are quite possibly already somewhat dehydrated by the time you feel thirsty. Dehydration can lead to constipation, an increase in body temperature, headaches, fuzzy thinking, lethargy, and an increase in your risk for kidney stones and bladder infections.

In addition to the physical benefits of water, the emotional benefits are wonderful. A shower, sauna, or bath can relax the body and mind, increase blood flow to soothe the nerves, calm digestion, and relieve joint or muscle pain. I have a friend who imagines the water washing away all the stresses of the day in the shower.

"Hydrotherapy" refers to using water to relieve pain, revitalize, and maintain or restore health. Hydrotherapy, of course, has been around for a long time. In fact, the first of the ten "domains of the spa," as defined by the International Spa Association, is "The Waters." "The Waters" actually find their roots in ancient civilizations. The Greeks enjoyed a variety of baths as early as 500 BC, and the Roman Empire continued the tradition for over two hundred years. Today our spas are a combination of ancient traditions and modern technology, but they still focus around the healing properties of water.

A walk beside a lake, river, or stream gets you away from the hustle and bustle of city life and into natural settings. There is a harmony and peace in nature that soothes the mind and soul. The rhythmic sounds of the ocean tide are relaxing and soothing. When I am feeling out of sync, I let my mind return to a particularly beautiful day on a small, quiet beach in Kona, Hawaii, where my family and I spent the day relaxing, playing on the beach, and listening to the soothing sounds of the ocean. This memory is one that I use to calm my mind and one that I use as a replacement for negative thoughts. Numerous relaxation CDs are available that incorporate the sounds of water and tides into them.

Service

One of the most healing and beneficial activities that we can become involved in is serving others. A crucial part of achieving balance in our lives involves finding our spirituality. This is a somewhat touchy topic to many, and as soon as it arises, we often fear being "preached" to. I appreciate Chapman's definition of spirituality. L. Chapman in 1987 in the *American Journal of Health Promotion* defined spirituality as "the ability to discover and express your purpose in life; to learn how to experience love, joy, peace and fulfillment; and to help yourself and others achieve their full potential."

Doing this begins with developing self-awareness, which is the ability to discover and live by who we are on the inside, regardless of the hustle and bustle of everyday life. You can begin by asking yourself "Who am I and what do I stand for?" Ekhart Tolle in *A New Earth: Awakening to Your Life's Purpose* recounts the story of a schoolteacher in her mid-forties who had been given only a short time to live. It was not until this point in her life that she was able to find the "stillness" within that she never new existed in her busy life as a schoolteacher. He tells us "you are never more essentially, more deeply yourself than when you are still." Incorporating precious moments into your hectic lifestyle to experience your "stillness" on a daily basis is a necessity today for long-term health and inner peace.

When you have found your own stillness, you are then able to move beyond yourself and connect with others in a serving capacity. Ralph Waldo Emerson said, "It is one of the most beautiful compensations of this life that no man can sincerely try to help another without helping himself." Providing service for others and volunteering your time not only allows you to meet new people and share your skills and talents, but it allows you to effect change and have a positive impact on your community, to gain a sense of achievement through championing a cause. It is a chance to give something back. If you take a moment to examine your life, you can probably see that you are already reaching out in your home, in your community, and in the lives of others. It is important that you acknowledge the incredible service you do, the impact you have on those around you, and the spiritual dimension that you add to your own life through this service.

Strategy #7

1. One of the first steps in changing your life is to be self-aware. It is through self-awareness that you identify and change the underlying core beliefs that either drive destructive behaviors or create happiness. Start by analyzing your interests and skills, your strengths and weaknesses, your fears and dreams, your needs and values. Identify the qualities you value in others, and list the qualities that your friends would value in you. When you have begun to develop self-awareness, explore answers to the following deeper questions: Who am I? Why am I here? What is my purpose in life? How can I help others to fulfill their destinies?

2. Find your "stillness." You may find your stillness when you are enjoying nature, during meditation in the quiet morning hours in your home, while reading religious texts or other spiritual material, and during those times when your mind is free of outside burdens and cares.

3. Examine your life. List those ways you are currently serving others in your home, your community, and your work. Celebrate the difference you make in the lives of others. If you find that this is an area where you are lacking, look for more opportunities to provide service to those in need either on your own or through programs in your community.

Chapter 10: Eliminate Detrimental Behaviors

There are two kinds of habits: doing habits and not doing habits.

—T. Harv Eker

We all have behaviors or strategies in place to deal with stress, whether we think we do or not. Some of our strategies are beneficial—those behavioral strategies that have long-term positive effects on our stress. Other strategies are detrimental—those behaviors that temporarily reduce our stress but have long-term negative effects. As we discuss some of these detrimental strategies, check your repertoire of coping mechanisms to see if you use any of these detrimental behaviors in your battle against stress.

Caffeine and Nicotine

Two highly addictive behaviors and very popular methods of coping with stress are drinking coffee and smoking cigarettes. While their short-term benefits can seem instantaneous, their long-term consequences can be devastating. Caffeine, a stimulant found in coffee, black tea, colas, and chocolate, chemically induces the "fight or flight" response in your body. So, if you feel stressed already, caffeine will only compound the problem. Caffeine and nicotine are powerful vasoconstrictors that decrease blood flow to the brain. Long-term, these substances decrease brain activity and make you need more to get the same effect. When you quit smoking, blood flow to your brain increases, but if you have been a chronic smoker there is an overall marked decrease in activity. Brain scans of long-time drinkers and smokers show marked deterioration in brain activity and have inspired many patients to change their ways.

In addition to their effects on the brain, caffeine and nicotine are also notorious for causing irritability, stomach problems, sleep difficulties, and anxiety.

Alcohol

Alcohol is frequently used as a tool to reduce stress, but unlike some of the beneficial tools we have discussed in previous chapters that sharpen your mind and body, alcohol reduces your accurate perception of reality by slowing certain functions in some parts of the brain. Alcohol can also irritate the gastrointestinal tract, cause hangovers, and inhibit sleep.

Davis, Eschelman, and McKay, in their book *The Relaxation and Stress Reduction Handbook*, state that "Although some research indicates that a drink a day may increase longevity, reliance on alcohol to deal with daily life is a dangerous practice." Alcoholic beverages are high in calories and low in nutrients. Excess alcohol depletes B vitamins, alters blood sugar, elevates blood pressure, and disrupts relationships.

But, you may be thinking, *I've heard that wine actually has beneficial effects on the body.* Dr. Mehmet Oz has recently written about the benefits of grapes in making your arteries more flexible and open. The equivalent of 1 1/4 cups of grapes (only 75 calories) can increase blood flow through the arteries. Yes, we have heard about the benefits of fermented grapes for years, but why not get some of those benefits in a pure, natural form with less calories and without the slurred speech and inappropriate behavior? Always keep in mind that drugs alter the brain's normal reward circuit, making it harder to feel pleasure without help.

Financial Misspending

Of course another of our great stressors in life is money—or, in many cases, the lack of it. Almost all of us have financial concerns. Financial stresses are not reserved for the poor or unemployed. If proper planning and self-control are not carried out, those of all economic situations can suffer in this area. If you struggle in this area, keep watch for workshops and seminars on budgeting and financial planning. Carefully chosen websites can have good counsel and sample budget forms for you to use. There are also numerous books on the subject that can be used as important resources. Don't be afraid or embarrassed to seek help.

The first step, as it is with almost everything we have discussed in this book, is to have a plan. Take the steps to create a meaningful budget or spending plan. I think the steps in the process will be quite universal no matter what guidelines you use as a resource.

1. Prioritize your long-term and short-term spending goals. Clearly specify wants versus needs, and ensure that you are not overspending on wants at the sacrifice of your needs. Make sure all of this is clearly written down and recorded.

2. Make a list of all your expenses in a month. Be sure to include yearly expenses like taxes, insurance, and vacations as well.

3. Estimate your income from all sources in a month.

4. Compare your income with your expenses. This can be the difficult part—especially if your expenses exceed your income. In this situation, your best options are to cut lower-priority items out of your budget or increase your income by taking a second job or finding a higher-paying job.

5. Develop and stick to a spending plan. Carefully examine your spending categories, and keep track of how much you spend in each of these areas.

6. Continually reexamine your plan and your spending habits. Effective budgeting takes time, patience, and practice.

Slow down

A number of years ago when I was teaching grade four, I had one of my students come running excitedly to me first thing Friday morning and announce, "Guess what our family is doing tonight!" With the amount of enthusiasm he was displaying, I assumed it must be pretty spectacular—a trip to Disneyland perhaps? When I asked what exciting thing they had planned, he replied, "We're staying home!" What a profound reflection on the "busyness" of our lives. We jam our lives full of commitments and activities. We wear our busyness on our chest like it is some kind of badge of honor. We take pride in the fact that our schedules are full and our lives are a constant whirlwind. We compare ourselves to others and feel an inward pleasure if we have taken on more than our neighbors or friends, if our children are involved in more sports or more activities than the other children in the neighborhood or school. Rosenfeld, Wise, and Coles, in their book *The Overscheduled Child*, tell us the following:

> Children whose every moment is scheduled and structured because their parents want them to have the benefit of everything the world has to offer may have difficulty learning how to be alone, and at peace, with themselves. And that may be the highest price we pay for micromanagement. Because the parents are so uneasy being quiet with themselves, because they insist that they must always run faster on their child's behalf, because they are afraid to let themselves be reflective and hear what they actually think or enjoy their own fantasies, they guarantee that their children will be racing like greyhounds, forever in the pursuit of mechanical bunnies they get oh-so-close to but never catch.

Some of the saddest stories from children, spouses, and friends reflect a desire just to be alone and talk with loved ones, but because we are so wrapped up in our own busyness, our relationships suffer from a lack of time and effort invested.

Ruminating

Are you a ruminator? Martin Seligman, in his fascinating book *Learned Optimism*, refers to people who mull over bad events as "ruminators." I have to confess that I am a ruminator. There have been certain events in my life—or, more specifically, events in the lives of my children—that have taken years for me to let go. For ruminators, any reminder of the original event sets the mind off on a long sequence of negative thoughts. This happens frequently to a ruminator, and it can often be difficult for the individual to distract him or herself or leave those particular thoughts.

In the past I have made conscientious, desperate efforts to change my thought patterns. I was aware of how detrimental they were to me, and I was fully aware of their presence, but I still struggled to get rid of them. I have made great improvements in this area, but I am still working on immediate recognition of the ruminating thoughts. As soon as I become aware, I verbally or in my mind make a command: Stop! Stop thoughts! I will not allow you in my mind! You are not worthy to occupy my thoughts! I will then redirect my thoughts by looking at the event from a positive perspective (because I feel strongly that we need to change the way we explain the bad events in our lives), and then I redirect my thoughts to a completely different topic.

I actually have a set of calming, wonderful experiences that have happened in my life that I am able to plug into my thoughts to replace the negative ones. Try making a list of the happiest moments or days in your life—relive those memories in your mind, look at pictures or write them down so you are able recall every detail—and have those memories ready to access when you need to redirect your thinking.

Withdrawal

Another of my favorite strategies when I am under extensive stress or going through a difficult challenge is to withdraw completely from the world. Having time to oneself is not in and of itself a negative, but withdrawing for extended periods of time and removing yourself from loved ones and the very support you may need during these difficult times does not always benefit you. If you are like me in this area, reread Chapter 3 and reinforce the importance of relationships in your life, the importance of serving others and of looking beyond your own needs to the needs of those around you. As you examine the detrimental behaviors in your life, remember that your focus needs to be on creating new behaviors rather than focusing on negative behaviors—focus on new behaviors, new goals, and new choices.

Strategy #8

1. Make a list of three of your most detrimental coping behaviors.

2. List three beneficial strategies that could replace these behaviors.

3. For three weeks, work daily on creating a new habit or strategy to cope with your stress.

My detrimental behaviors

1.

2.

3.

Replacement strategies

1.

2.

3.

Chapter 11: Organization and Time Management

Things that matter most must never be at the mercy of things which matter least.

—Goethe

A major cause of stress in both our home lives and our workplaces is a lack of organization and time management skills. Devoting sincere time and effort into organizing our schedules, our homes, our desks, our calendars can save us a great deal of anxiety. And when we lack the appropriate strategies and tools to organize ourselves, we often engage in probably the most common cause of stress in our lives . . . procrastination. Procrastination holds us back from achieving our goals in the "Sisyphus effect."

In Greek mythology, we find the story of Sisyphus, the founder and king of the city of Corinth. Sisyphus was notorious for being the most cunning knave on earth. His trickery and deceit finally caught up with him, and for his crimes against the gods he was condemned to an eternity of hard labor. But it was not just any hard labor; it was frustrating and unfulfilling hard labor. His assignment was to roll a great boulder to the top of a hill. Only every time Sisyphus, by the greatest of exertion and toil, attained the summit, the boulder rolled back down again.

Have you ever felt like Sisyphus? You struggle and try so hard, and yet you never quite succeed? What is holding you back? What will help you finally push your boulder over the hill? Often when we have committed ourselves to make changes in our lives, we find ourselves rolling the boulder up the hill, but we are often held back by some force in our lives that seems to keep us in our comfort zones of mediocrity, of addiction, of unhappiness. Find what your barrier is, and make a conscious effort to overcome it. Perhaps your barriers lie in the areas of organization and time management. Let me share with you what I call the Seven S's of Organization and Time Management:

1. **S**et and Share Goals:

   Make conscious choices about your future—don't just sit back and let it happen. Don't just expect good things and great opportunities to drop in your lap, make them happen!
   a. Put your goal very specifically and clearly down on paper. (A goal is just a wish until you write it down!)
   b. Set a deadline for completion. This builds in a sense of urgency and accountability.
   c. Carefully plan out the steps necessary to achieve your goal, and set deadlines.
   d. Get started. It has been said that the hardest part of getting started . . . is getting started!
   e. Share your goal. This makes it real and builds in the accountability of having someone who knows what you are working toward.
   f. Pay the price! Be patient, be purposeful, and be persistent.

2. **S**tipulate Priorities:

   Renew your energy and your thoughts. Set your priorities, and deeply commit yourself to a happy, successful, and productive day. Then, each evening, measure the quality of your day by accounting for what you accomplished. Outline several questions that will measure your success. My four questions are 1) Whose life did you positively influence today? 2) Who did you pass judgment on? Why? 3) What positive family connection did you make? 4) What steps did you take to move your business forward?

3. **S**agacious (Wise) Scheduling:

   Once you have set your priorities, it becomes easier to schedule your day. Remember the 10/90 rule. This rule says that the first 10 percent of time you spend planning and organizing your work before you start will save you as much as 90 percent of the time it takes to get the job done once you get started. Set aside time each morning to sit down and plan your day. When setting your schedule, build in plans to limit your interruptions—phone calls, emails, drive-by shootings (colleagues or friends who stop in to "shoot" the breeze). Limit mindless activities like watching endless hours of television, surfing the internet, or having long, gossipy phone conversations.

4. **S**hortcuts:

Use incredible caution in utilizing shortcuts. Taking shortcuts saves time in the short term, but often it costs you in the long term. One of my mottos is, "Do it right the first time." Why waste time having to redo tasks when slowing down, putting in careful thought, and planning can help you do it right the first time? Try to handle paperwork and other such tasks only once.

5. **S**top Procrastinating:

Procrastination involves delaying important higher-priority tasks for less important, lower-priority tasks. When we examine the causes of stress in our lives, procrastination could very well be responsible for more anxiety, stress, and underachievement than any other single factor.

I feel like I am more than qualified to address this topic—if experience makes me qualified. In most of my life I am incredibly efficient and well-organized, but there are certain areas where procrastination seems to be the unconquerable foe. Take writing this book, for instance. My first challenge is to get myself into my office and sit at my computer so I am at least in a position to write. My next challenge is to focus on the task at hand. Often my routine follows this pattern: I need to get in and finish that chapter. I'll just finish this TV show, I'll just throw in a load of laundry, I'll just make a quick phone call first, and the list goes on. Then when I am seated at my computer,

I feel the need to check my email first or Google a few interesting topics. This morning I actually spent an hour on Amazon.com researching and ordering some important books that needed to be ordered. Then I might need to tidy up the study or find a DVD or book that might help inspire me. Just when I am ready to begin I need to let the dogs out, and as I walk through the kitchen I decide I should probably empty the dishwasher. You get the picture. So what is the answer to this perplexing problem?

I have several suggestions for reducing procrastination. (Notice I didn't say eliminating—that goal would set me up for certain failure!)

- Take the time to plan your day out in advance. Once your goals are set—create a mindset to succeed. Start seeing yourself as a person who takes action and gets things done. Dive into your tasks with a sense of urgency. Develop good habits. Complete your tasks. Create energy and focus. If you don't have complete focus, you don't have a clear vision of what you want to accomplish, and then it becomes easy to procrastinate because you don't know where you are going. I am the queen of making and crossing off items on a list. I feel such a sense of accomplishment each time I can cross off a task. Once your list is made, stick to it! Then as your day progresses, keep asking yourself: what is the most valuable use of my time right now? And once again, when you decide what that is, do it. This is all part of prioritizing your daily agenda.

- Keep your work area clear and have only those tasks at hand in front of you so you know exactly what to focus on. Get yourself quickly situated and get started. As you are working, talk yourself positively through it. Instead of telling yourself, "I hate this," "I can't do this," or "I'll never finish on time," be positive in your self-talk.

- Set small goals to help make a formidable task seem doable. For example, if you have two hours of work on the computer and you are having difficulty getting motivated, set a goal to spend fifteen minutes at work. Set a timer and work consistently through until it rings. Often the most difficult part of getting started is just that—getting started! And once you are able to get into the project you will often feel like sticking with it. And spending those two hours becomes easier.

- Examine carefully what is stopping you from getting started, sticking to it, or finishing a task. When you have identified the problem, address it. For example, if the television is a distraction, move it, unplug it, or set up a schedule with a maximum time limit—and stick to it.

- My last suggestion is to gauge your productivity. Really think about and examine how productive you are after a certain length of time, at certain times of the day, and plan your work accordingly. Perhaps you are most productive at 9 a.m. and are able to work for an hour without a break. Plan your hour-long task for that time. Perhaps after lunch you are less effective and require frequent breaks to stay awake and focused. Plan activities or work for that level of productivity. Always take the necessary breaks and eat properly so your energy levels are sustained and you can remain focused. If your eating habits are such that you have spikes and dips in your blood sugar, your focus may also dip and spike.

6. **S**ettle the Clutter:

The simple (or not so simple) task of organizing your workspace can free your mind to be more creative and productive, and help you become more efficient and effective in your day. A cluttered, unorganized work area can add more stress and distraction, and frustrate your efforts to accomplish your daily tasks. Try these strategies to achieve a more efficient working environment:

- Keep materials for only the project you are working on in front of you.

- Have a calendar and clock close to you.

- Purchase a filing cabinet and establish a system in which files are clearly labeled, color coded, and alphabetical.

- Have an in box and an out box for incoming and completed tasks.

- Read your mail and messages with a colored marker in hand. Highlight important deadlines, phone numbers, or events.

- Use a bound notebook or day planner instead of endless sticky notes.

- Reorganize your desk at the end of the day, and record what needs to be done tomorrow.

7. Secure Private Time:

   Purposefully schedule uninterrupted blocks of time each day to participate in a fun activity, read, meditate, or just relax in the tub. Find a quiet place and time to be isolated completely from distractions so that you can maximize your efficiency and have time to recharge your batteries.

Strategy #9

Try to incorporate the Seven S's into your life.

If you are serious about making permanent changes in this area of your life, I highly recommend Stephen Covey's *7 Habits of Highly Effective People*. The book and seminars are life changing.

Chapter 12: Workplace Stress

We don't see things as they are. We see things as we are.

—Anais Nin

Workplace stress is, just as the name suggests, stress that finds its roots in the workplace, where we find ourselves incurring the harmful effects of job demands. These harmful effects can be physical or emotional or both, and they can come from a number of different sources at work, which can make them difficult to address. Some of the stresses we experience are intrinsic to the job, some are caused by our relationships at work or the structure and climate of our place of employment, and some are caused by our own personalities, past experiences, and characteristics. Add to the mix the stresses we bring with us to work—our family problems, our financial worries, our health issues—and you see how complicated understanding and dealing with workplace stress can become.

The most common causes of work stress seem to be a lack of control over the work situation, work overload, unfair treatment, unsupportive or hostile coworkers, inadequate learning, and a lack of recognition. The National Institute for Occupational Safety and Health tells us that about one-third of workers report high levels of stress in their jobs, and about one-fourth of employees view their jobs as the number-one stressor in their lives. Stress in the workplace not only causes individual suffering and distress, but it also creates a substantial burden for our communities through health care costs, absenteeism from work, and lost productivity. It only makes sense that stressed workers are more likely to be unhealthy, poorly motivated, less productive, and less safe at work.

When we speak of workplace stress, it important to note that just like regular stress in our lives, some workplace stress is essential. A job with no challenges or stress could end up being boring, with no sense of accomplishment or fulfillment. Interestingly, work stress is not just caused by work overloads, but it also occurs when the job is too easy and presents little challenge. Robert Yerkes and John Dodson of Harvard University found that as stress increases, so does productivity—to a certain point. Once stress exceeds a certain level, productivity starts to decrease. You need to find your "zone" of productivity so that you can work most efficiently.

On that note, what can you do to help reduce workplace stress? My hope is that working through this book will have already given you numerous ideas on how to find balance and reduce stress in your home and work lives. Let me suggest five key areas to work on when addressing workplace stress specifically.

1. Be Self-Aware: How do you respond to your stressors at work? The more aware you are of your own triggers and biases, the more you read your reactions and monitor yourself emotionally during your interactions with others. Carefully think through and make a list of the things that create stress at work. List the situation, how it makes you feel (be very specific), what you are presently doing about it, and what you could or should be doing about it.

For example: Perhaps you have a toxic, complaining coworker at work. She makes you think negatively and dwell on what is wrong at work and what could go wrong at work. Presently you are buying into the negativity and contributing to the conversation and the toxic environment. Upon thinking about it you feel you should be removing yourself from that influence and those conversations. There are lots of positive things at work, and if there are things with which you are dissatisfied, you feel you should talk to someone who can do something about it—a manager or boss—rather than gossiping, backbiting, and being part of the problem instead of being a part of the solution.

2. Increase Your Organization and Time Management Skills: Chapter 10 addresses this topic in detail, please refer to that chapter.

3. Learn to Communicate Effectively and Develop Strong Conflict Resolution Skills: Often we can find the root of our stress in our relationships. Communicating effectively is essential in maintaining positive relationships. A rebellious child, an insensitive spouse, a controlling boss, or a competitive coworker can cause a great deal of stress. Three key ingredients in our relationships are to learn to listen effectively, forgive, and resolve conflicts. We discussed forgiveness in Chapter 2.

Learning to Listen

One of the most powerful principles I have learned in my life is Stephen Covey's fifth habit: Seek first to understand, then to be understood. Covey's ideas on empathetic listening are life-changing if we will study, practice, and apply this important skill.

As a school teacher for many years, I spent a great deal of time teaching reading, writing, and arithmetic, but I spent considerably less time teaching listening skills. In fact, I would think that very few of us have ever really had much training in the art of listening. We live in a very self-centered society, and this self-centeredness is reflected in our listening skills. We want to be understood first and foremost, no matter what the emotional cost. Covey tells us, "most people do not listen with the intent to understand, they listen with the intent to reply." Think carefully about that statement, and think about the last serious conversation you had with someone. Were you truly listening with an open heart and mind, and truly trying to understand their feelings and concerns; or was your mind busy searching your vast experience so that you could reply with advice and savory examples from your own life that would be helpful.

When was the last time you truly needed someone to just listen and understand, and they cut you off mid-sentence with words like "I know exactly how you feel," or "That's nothing—listen to my experience," or "You shouldn't feel like that." How helpful were those words of wisdom? Each of us has a deep-seated desire to truly be seen, to be heard, to be understood, and to be known and appreciated for ourselves.

Until we listen empathetically to someone, we do not have completely accurate information with which to work when trying to communicate or interact on any level. We do not have to have the same point of view as someone, and we don't have to agree with what they are saying—that is not what empathetic listening is. It is truly understanding them, trying to see things through their perspective and their experience. Then, and only then, can deep and full communication take place.

Consider your rebellious teenager. How often do you truly try to understand the message behind his or her behavior? Or do you immediately just jump in, pass judgment, share stories of when you were young, and try to "fix" him or her with your superior suggestions and knowledge?

Consider your "tyrant" boss. Before you jump in and start second-guessing his or her decisions and actions, perhaps you should consider seeing the situation from your boss's perspective.

Resolve Conflicts

Over 90 percent of conflict results from the way we define certain terms or words and how we interpret the information that we hear. Can you see the importance of empathetic listening again? Conflicts in the home and in the workplace provide a lot of the stress in our lives. So taking steps to understand and resolve conflicts will greatly benefit our physical and emotional well-being.

Conflicts need to be resolved early and quickly. When resolving conflicts, this principle can have a powerful influence: think, "Not yours or mine . . . but ours." Two simple steps can resolve most conflicts

Step 1: Each party states his or her side of the issue—your side and my side. Listen empathetically, and agree to restate the other's person's point of view to his or her satisfaction before making a new point of your own.

Step 2: Both parties need to agree to come up with a solution that is better than either "yours" or "mine"—an "ours" solution. In conflict resolution we need to remember that we are *not* trying to convince someone that our point of view is correct, and we are *not* trying to manipulate someone. We want to end up with an alternative solution that makes both parties happy. Not yours or mine . . . but ours. Remember the power of validating the other person's point of view. Words like "I really appreciate you bringing this concern forward" can be meaningful and powerful bridge builders.

1. Develop Positive Thinking and Increase Productivity: Remember the importance of your thoughts in engaging the stress response. This can have a huge impact on your workplace stress.

2. Learn to Make Efficient, Effective Decisions: An essential skill in time management and problem solving is the ability to use efficient and effective decision-making tools. When making decisions, you must first carefully analyze the type of decision, and then you can more carefully take action. Knowing how to make quick, effective decisions can greatly reduce your stress at work and increase your credibility as a manager, employee, or leader of any type. The following are ways to carefully analyze a situation in which a decision needs to be made:

   a. Does your decision require listing your choices in an order of what will give you the biggest benefits? For example: If you are embarking on house renovations, and you have four projects pending, your best decision-making technique may be to consider which renovations will provide the biggest benefits. The roof is leaking, the bathroom plumbing doesn't work, the curtains are ugly, the stove is on its last legs, and the furniture it old and beat-up. Replacing the furniture first may not be the best choice when it is raining outside and the sewer is backed up!

b. Does the decision require weighing the pros, cons, and implications of a decision?

For example: If you are deciding whether or not you should go on a Caribbean Cruise, you can make a chart and list the pros, cons, and interesting things about embarking on such an adventure.

c. Do you need to decide whether or not a change is necessary?

For example: As a family you have outgrown your present home and you are deciding whether you need to buy a new home. Listing the cost associated with the new house and the benefits involved would be an effective way of handling this situation.

d. Are you making a decision that requires you to analyze a problem from a number of different perspectives?

For example: You are contemplating returning to university or college to obtain another degree.

Look at the problem creatively: what are some ways that you could come up with the time and money to pursue such a decision?

Look at the problem defensively: why might this decision not work, what could go wrong, what are the negative aspects of this decision?

Look at the problem optimistically: what are the benefits and where is the value in making this decision?

Look at the decision intuitively: often we ignore what our "gut" is telling us. Take the time to listen to your emotions and feelings on the decision.

And finally, look at big picture: examine all the information you have thought about, recorded, and researched.

Let me finish this chapter by speaking quite honestly. If you have assessed your job stress and attempted to alleviate it without avail, you might just want to find a new job. Maybe the stress is a sign that it is time for a change—time to return to school, time to look for something more challenging, or time to look for something more interesting. Change can often be a door to great opportunity.

Chapter 13: College Stress

To do anything less than your best is to sacrifice the gift.

—*Steve Prefontaine*

The college experience. Exciting, challenging . . . stressful.

My college experience turned out significantly different from what I had expected. As I prepared to leave my home in Coaldale, Alberta, Canada, at eighteen to attend the University of Minnesota in Minneapolis, I had no idea what adventures awaited me. I had left my home of six thousand people and one stoplight to attend a university with a population of sixty-five thousand students with the intention of taking in the college experience that we all hear about. I wanted to share nights out with roommates, stay up all night cramming for exams, experience an awkward blind date or two, cheer for the college football team, and then leave four years later with my degree in hand and a lot of memories. Instead I ended up with so much more. One student visa turned into a green card, two amazing internships, one marriage, two wedding receptions in two different countries, and a last-minute move across the United States and here I am. A long way from where I began but worth every unexpected minute.

So often during my time in university I listened to friends panic with anxiety before a test or hyperventilate as they watched the clock tick away the hours before a huge project was due. Through my unconventional experiences I learned how to maximize my time and use the skills I had already developed not only to do well in my classes but to utilize the opportunities that came my way throughout college as well.

There's really no set formula, no easy way to an A, and no one right answer for everyone. I firmly believe, however, that if you are willing to take the time to implement some of the strategies that I have found useful, your experience in college can be as successful as you want it to be. The following are steps that outline a plan for success.

Have a Plan

1. **Use some type of a planning system.** I have a planner. It has a green cover, and that green cover is smattered with pink and purple and blue polka dots. Not very professional, and probably not the most fashionable accessory, but it has my life in it. You may not be a big fan of carrying around a planner. You may lose it. Find out what is right for you. Whether it's punching in due dates on your Blackberry, or using Post-It notes, or maybe even just a lined notebook. Just make sure you have some sort of accountability for what you are working on and that somewhere, in some place, your schedule is written down. Those five to ten minutes of effort will save you so much more in productivity later on.

2. **Map out your semester**. Staying on top of ever-mounting assignments, keeping up with friends, and juggling work or family can be a huge load. It takes a plan. For me, that meant having something in writing. I had my planner with me at all times, and on the first day of each semester I looked over the syllabus and wrote down every assignment, every exam, and every due date. This took approximately five to ten minutes for each class. In no time at all I had my entire semester mapped out, and in this way I could keep track of everything to do with school. After that, if any changes were made or extensions granted, I made sure to write it down in my planner.

3. **Create weekly plans.** Every Sunday I prepared for the coming week by looking through my planner to see what would be due, what exams I had to study for, or what papers I needed to start writing. By having a weekly plan I was never surprised by an assignment

or test and never felt rushed or stressed out to finish something on time.

Avoid Procrastination

We all procrastinate. I have fought with it nearly every day of each semester. In Chapter 10 we outlined general ideas for fighting procrastination, and here are some that are specific to college life:

1. **Be realistic**. Putting off assignments, having a slow day, or wanting to sleep in instead of studying will happen. Your goal should be simply to try to make sure it doesn't happen too often. What I find most useful in this area leads into the second idea, make a list.

2. **Make a list.** Each day make a list of the assignments or tasks that you need to accomplish, whether it's for that day or for the week. Now, look over what you've written. Chances are there will be a few items on the list that you are absolutely not looking forward to. Do these first! This could be the best piece of advice I give. If you can take these items off your list and get them out of the way, your day can only get better after that.

3. **Take the question mark out of your sentences.** Here's what I mean by that. One Saturday morning I woke up to a beautiful spring morning. The sun was shining, and my bed was welcoming me to stay and enjoy it for just a few more minutes. I thought to myself, "Do I really need to study today?" And here was my response: "Well I could study this morning, but I'm sure I'll have time tomorrow, and besides, I have so many things around the house that I could be doing, and I'm sure my husband needs me to stick around. No, I think I'll stay in bed." This is how it works nearly every time. I found the common denominator to my unproductive days was that there was a question mark at the end of my sentence. If I had woken up instead with the thought,

"Today I am going to study," there would have been no opportunity for my little inner debate. And this is my advice for you. Take that question mark out! Don't allow yourself to rationalize and debate whether or not your schoolwork is a priority.

Find Your Place

I can't tell you how many times I made a goal to study at home on the weekends only to find myself momentarily distracted by the newest month's picture on the wall calendar. As I ponder this new picture I start to realize that the wall color is really getting on my nerves. And maybe the carpet should be vacuumed. And is that frame completely tilted, or is it just me? The point here is that we need to understand our limitations.

1. **Decide what motivates and what distracts you.** I know that I will not get work done if I am in my house, if I am with my friends, or if I am in a noisy area. I will do nearly anything to get out of doing work. If this means doing laundry or taking out the garbage, I will do it, all in the search for distractions. So here's the solution.

2. **Find a place that works for you**. For me, that involves finding a place where I can be alone and where I feel motivated. That place is a small cubby in the basement of the library on campus. It is in a corner where nearly no one frequents, and it is far enough away from any of the other desks that I am out of earshot when some student decides he or she wants to disturb the silence by eating a huge bag of baby carrots.

3. **Force yourself to get there.** If you can find that place where you can work completely undisturbed, then you don't need to worry about distractions or getting yourself motivated. Your mind will become wired so that it knows that when you come back to your special

study area, that means work. If you can take that first difficult step of deciding to get yourself to your place, then the rest will fall into place.

Cultivate Supportive Relationships

Part of your college experience should involve developing and maintaining supportive relationships. There are several important relationships that are crucial to cultivate.

1. **Get to know professors and professional contacts.** I had the opportunity to be taught by incredible professors who took the time to speak with me one on one. I learned so much from them. Your professors are an untapped resource. They have a wealth of experience, usually in the field that you want to enter. Your professor may not be someone that you like or someone that you agree with all the time, but at the end of the day they are the ones who control your grades. If you walk into class with the right attitude, regardless of your personal feelings, it will be a positive learning experience. So make an effort to be respectful and take those opportunities that are given to seek out a mentor in your professor or in professionals who work within the field in which you are interested. As a student you have opportunities and access to resources that no one else does.

2. **Surround yourself with good friends.** College is a time of freedom and escape from parents and authority figures. Don't let this newfound freedom and excitement take away from the real reason you are attending classes. It is important to have friends who are fun to be with and who know how to have a good time. But, more importantly, it is essential that you surround yourself with friends who are going to set an example for you of hard work and dedication. These are friends who are not going to let you waste your time and money

on a college education while you party it away. These relationships are not relationships of convenience or fun, but they will be the most lasting. Understand the difference between short-term happiness and long-term goals. In the short-term you may find it's easier to sleep through your morning classes and just get by with the minimum amount of effort. In the long run, however, you will find yourself with an un-repairable GPA and falling prospects for career opportunities after the fun of college.

3. **If possible, maintain close family ties.** Family comes in many forms. I always had my mom and my husband to lean on, but for many, grandparents, siblings, or good friends can be that unconditional source of support. Work to keep these relationships even if you are separated by distance or time.

Enjoy!

You should enjoy your college experience, and it's important to learn this now. I, however, came to this understanding in my senior year. Before this time I was so preoccupied with just staying on top of all of the work and unexpected changes that I hadn't thought about all of the opportunities I was missing. These four years are a time of learning and growth, a time when you are generally uninhibited by responsibilities that will come later with a career and a family. Take this opportunity to increase self-awareness. Manage your time wisely, get organized, learn new skills, and develop relationships that are supportive and lasting. And, most of all, enjoy!

Chapter 14: Develop a Plan

Concerning all acts of initiative and creation, there is one elementary truth—that the moment one definitely commits oneself, then Providence moves, too.

—*Johann Wolfgang Von Goethe*

My daughter rode public transportation to get to the university every day, and I had the chance to ride with her on several occasions. I love public transportation, not only for its environmental benefits, but I never worried about her traveling on bad roads or fighting traffic jams. When the train had reached its final destination, my daughter transferred onto a bus for the final leg of her journey. A woman's voice announced through the train, "The end of the line. As far as we go." Often in our lives we feel we have reached the end of the line and gone as far as we can go. So here's the lesson from public transport: If I continue to sit on the train after that announcement I will progress no further. In fact, I will actually start backtracking and return to previous destinations—perhaps revisiting old habits, reliving past failures or disappointments, finding past friends or associates who may have been toxic to my emotional and physical state. Instead, get off the train and jump on the bus; find another way to get to your destination, to achieve your goals, to keep progressing and moving forward.

Our lives are full of roadblocks—divorce, disappointment, death, discouragement, job loss, defiant children. They may slow you down, but don't let them stop you completely. Take a detour! And if there seems to be no detour, no road to where you need to get, build it! And if there is water in the way, swim across. You have the tools now! Or better yet, build a bridge so others can follow in your footsteps.

I hope our message in this book has become very clear. We need to take care of ourselves—really take care of ourselves—so that we are healthy and strong both emotionally and physically to carry on. It's no secret that we live in an increasingly stressful environment. Our own wellness is the key to being able to be effective in our homes, our families, and our workplaces. Acknowledging, understanding, and dealing with stress is essential.

Fascinating new research outlines the sensitivities of both fetuses and young children to the stress in their parents' lives, as well as the developmental difficulties that can present themselves as a result of that stress. Studies increasingly focus on stress as the root of most illnesses, and serious disruptions appear in both homes and workplaces due to mishandled stress. We need to utilize the positive stress in our lives to enhance our personal growth and spur us on to greater achievements, and through informed choices we can learn to counteract the negative effects that stress can place on us. By achieving balance in these five key areas—physical, emotional, intellectual, behavioral, and spiritual—we can gain a renewed sense of happiness and well being, and an energy that comes from living a stress-enhanced rather than stress-depleted lifestyle.

We've looked at a number of stress management strategies and areas in your life to examine. At the end of each chapter you have had an opportunity to try out some of these ideas. Now it is time to put this new knowledge and approach into an action plan. I would like you to utilize two plans—a short-term plan and a long-term plan. The short-term plan will be the "Six-Second Stress Stabilizers" you designed in Chapter 8. Use this in the midst of your stressful day and during stressful situations. The Stress Management Plan exercise below is a long-term exercise that will help you create a powerful visual picture of managing stress optimally.

Commit to following through with your plan and build accountability and rewards into it. Write your goals down and keep them displayed where you can view them several times a day. Share your goals with a friend or family member—someone who will support and encourage you in your endeavor. And be willing to sacrifice your old ways to achieve a new way of thinking, reacting, and living.

Nature teaches us such fascinating lessons. I'm sure many of you are familiar with the Chinese bamboo tree. Bamboo trees can grow faster than any plant on earth. They can grow six or more inches in a day—up to eighty feet in a growing season. Another interesting fact is that they only flower every 60–120 years. When planted, the Chinese bamboo tree shows no growth for five years. Then in the fifth year it grows at unprecedented rates. For five years it develops a foundation and support system that will sustain the record growth.

And so it is with our lives. Great achievements and great growth are the result of patiently building self-discipline, self-awareness, and character to sustain the growth necessary to help you achieve your goals, dreams, and aspirations. Be patient, be persistent, and be proactive. The benefits will be well worth the effort!

So, will you sink or swim? Next time you are drowning in stress, pull out a few strategies, float to the top, and swim to the shore. You have the knowledge and the confidence to take control of the situation and your stress. Happy swimming!

My Stress Management Plan

Identifying my life stressors. Thoughtfully identify what is causing the stress in your life (work, home, personal). Be as specific as possible.

    1. _____

    2. _____

    3. _____

    4. _____

How is stress impacting me? Identify your body's physiological response to stress.

    1. _____

    2. _____

    3. _____

    4. _____

How am I coping currently? What physical, intellectual, emotional, behavioral, or spiritual strategies do I presently utilize?

    1. _____

    2. _____

    3. _____

    4. _____

Steps I can take to achieve:

Behavioral Balance

    1. _____

    2. _____

    3. _____

Intellectual/Cognitive Balance

1. _____
2. _____
3. _____

Spiritual Balance

1. _____
2. _____
3. _____

Emotional Balance

1. _____
2. _____
3. _____

Physical Balance

1. _____
2. _____
3. _____

References

Bennett, M. P., Zeller, J. M., Rosenberg, L., & McCann, J. (2003). "The Effect of Mirthful Laughter on Stress and Natural Killer and Cell Activity." *Alternative Therapy Health Medicine*, Mar–Apr; 9(2): 38–45.

Campbell, D. (1997). *The Mozart Effect: Tapping the Power of Music to Heal the Body, Strengthen the Mind, and Unlock the Creative Spirit*. New York: Avon Books.

Cannon, W. B. (1929). *Bodily Changes in Pain, Hunger, Fear and Rage* (2nd ed.). New York: Harpers Torchbooks.

Carlson, R. (2006). *You Can Be Happy No Matter What: Principles for Keeping Life in Perspective*. Novato, CA: New World Library.

Covey, S. R. (1989). *The Seven Habits of Highly Effective People: Restoring the Character Ethic*. New York: Simon & Schuster.

Davis, M., Eschelman, E. R., & McKay, M. (2008). *The Relaxation and Stress Workbook* (5th ed.). Oakland, CA: New Harbinger Publications.

Dew, S. (2005). *If Life Were Easy, It Wouldn't Be Hard: And Other Reassuring Truths*. Salt Lake City: Deseret Book.

Eker, T. H. (2005). *Secrets of the Millionaire Mind: Mastering the Inner Game of Wealth*. New York: Harper Business.

Frost, P. J. (2003). *Toxic Emotions at Work*. Boston, MA: Harvard Business School Press.

Goleman, D. (1994). *Emotional Intelligence: Why It Can Matter More than I. O.* New York: Bantam Books.

Jorde-Bloom, P. (1982). *Avoiding Burnout: Strategies for Managing Time, Space, and People in Early Childhood Education*. Washington, DC: Acropolis Books, Ltd.

Rosenfeld, A. & Wise, N. (2000). *The Overscheduled Child: Avoiding the Hyper-Parenting Trap*. New York: St. Martin's Griffin.

Seligman, M. E. P. (2006). *Learned Optimism: How to Change Your Mind and Your Life.* New York: Vintage Books.

Selye, H. (1956). *The Stress of Life.* New York: McGraw-Hill.

Tolle, E. (2005). *A New Earth: Awakening to Your Life's Purpose.* London: Plume.

Wooten, P. (1996). "Humor: An Antidote for Stress." *Holistic Nursing Practice.* Jan; 10(2): 49–56.

The Yerkes-Dodson law was first published in R. M. Yerkes & J. D. Dodson. (1909). "The Relation of Strength of Stimulus to Rapidity of Habit-Formation." *Journal of Comparative Neurology and Psychology,* 18, 459–482.

Printed in the United States
by Baker & Taylor Publisher Services